Grand Diplôme Cooking Course

Volume 18

Grand Diplôme Cooking Course

A Danbury Press Book

The Danbury Press

a division of Grolier Enterprises, Inc.

Robert B. Clarke   Publisher

This book has been adapted from the Grand Diplôme Cooking Course, originally published by Purnell Cookery, U.S.A.

Purnell Grand Diplôme Editorial Board

Rosemary Hume and Muriel Downes Principals, London Cordon Bleu Cookery School, England

Anne Willan	Editor
Eleanor Noderer	Associate Editor
Sheryl Julian	Assistant Editor
John Paton	Managing Editor
José Northey	Co-ordinating Editor
Peter Leather	Art Editor
Charles F. Turgeon	Wine Consultant

All recipes have been tested either at the Cordon Bleu Cookery School in London or in our U.S. test kitchens.

Note: all recipe quantities in this book serve 4 people unless otherwise stated.

Contents

From the Editor

Scale the heights of **French Haute Cuisine** in Volume 18 of your Grand Diplôme Cooking Course. With the knowledge you have gained from the past Volumes, you'll have no trouble achieving the sublimely smooth sauce or the shimmering crystal-clear aspic needed for dishes like suprêmes de poisson Parisienne and filet de boeuf en gelée bouquetière. Impress your guests with chicken à la Kiev, stuffed with delicious hot herb butter, or a splendid hot chocolate soufflé, puffed high in its dish. Equally elegant are **Classic Fish Dishes** — poach a whole salmon and serve it hot with a fennel-flavored velouté sauce or stuff fresh trout with a shrimp mousse and serve them cold with a spicy mayonnaise.

Recreate the glories of the French buffet table with **Chaudfroids and Galantines** intended particularly for grand occasions. With the help of the Cordon Bleu Cookery School in London, you'll easily master such specialties as galantine of duck — boned and stuffed with veal and truffles, then poached before coating with a rich brown sauce and sherry-flavored aspic.

Elaborate **European Gâteaux** are the traditional ending to lavish cold buffets. Marvelously rich melting confections, irridescent with icings and laden with nuts, they include creations like doboz torte — six cake layers filled with chocolate butter cream frosting and coated with caramel. And everyone is sure to succumb to the temptations of **Bombes, Parfaits and Iced Desserts**. Who could resist a colorful molded bombe, striped with several favorite flavors of ice cream, or the perfect parfait, layered with meringues or ladyfingers and topped with fruit and whipped cream?

Our final **Menus** are also on a grand scale. Dishes like homemade consommé madrilène, saddle of lamb garnished with colorful vegetables and a flaky mille feuilles filled with fresh strawberries and cream will test your cooking powers as well as the palates of your guests. The golden wedding menu of roast stuffed duck in aspic and the croquembouche gâteau is ideal for other occasions as well, so why not celebrate and cook your way to graduation from Grand Diplôme?

Congratulations and Bon Appétit !

Anne Willan

Dinner party menu for ten includes shrimp bisque, roast saddle of lamb, pineapple en surprise with spun sugar and various petits fours

THE EPITOME OF ELEGANCE

Shrimp Bisque

Roast Saddle of Lamb Jardinière
Jardinière Platter

Pineapple en Surprise
with Spun Sugar
Assorted Petits Fours

〰️

White wine – Medium Dry Sherry (Amontillado)
Red wine – Pauillac (Médoc)
or Cabernet Sauvignon (California)
White wine – Sauternes (Bordeaux)
or Sweet Sauvignon Blanc (California)

This menu combines classic French dishes in a superlative dinner for ten people. Fresh shrimp bisque is followed by luxurious roast saddle of lamb with a jardinière platter of vegetables. The spectacular dessert is a pineapple filled with orange sherbet, garnished with spun sugar and served with homemade petits fours.

Wine with the soup is not the usual thing, but a glass of sherry can be very welcome with seafood bisques. Any good quality medium dry sherry will do, but Spain's classic Amontillado is best. For the lamb, choose a red Bordeaux from the Médoc district – any of the great château wines from the town of Pauillac, or for an American alternative, a Cabernet Sauvignon. A dessert wine can add a pleasant finishing touch to so elegant a meal; try a French Sauternes or a sweet Sauvignon Blanc from California's Livermore Valley.

TIMETABLE

Day before
Make soup but do not add shrimp butter; store, covered, in refrigerator.
Make croûtons, if using, and keep in plastic bag.
Make orange sherbet and store in freezer.
Make petits fours and store in an airtight container.

Morning
Prepare and trim vegetables for jardinière platter; store in plastic bags in refrigerator. Peel potatoes and cover with cold water.
Cut pineapple, sprinkle slices with sugar and kirsch, cover tightly, and refrigerate.

Assemble ingredients for final cooking from 5:30 for dinner around 8 p.m.

You will find that **cooking times** given in the individual recipes for these dishes have sometimes been adapted in the timetable to help you when cooking and serving this menu as a party meal.

Order of Work
5:30
Set oven at moderately hot (375°F).
5:45
Depending on cooking time, prepare saddles of lamb and put in oven. Baste every 15–20 minutes.
6:40
Put potatoes to roast with lamb.
Arrange petits fours on a platter ready for serving.
6:50
Make spun sugar to decorate pineapple.
Cook cauliflower, onions and carrots for jardinière platter.
7:30
Cook Brussels sprouts, zucchini and mushrooms for jardinière platter.
7:45
Transfer saddles of lamb to serving platter and keep hot; transfer potatoes to serving dish and keep hot.
Make gravy; reheat vegetables, arrange on platter, add sauce and keep hot.
Heat soup but do not boil; stir in butter and add garnish. Transfer sherbet to refrigerator to soften it slightly.
8:00
Serve soup.
Between courses arrange pineapple en surprise on platter, fill with sherbet and decorate with spun sugar just before serving.

Appetizer

Shrimp Bisque

2 lb medium shrimps
10 tablespoons butter
1 small carrot, finely chopped
1 small onion, finely chopped
bouquet garni
1 cup white wine
¼ cup flour
2 quarts well-flavored chicken stock
salt and pepper
¼ cup light cream
2 tablespoons brandy, sherry or Madeira
4 slices of white bread, crusts removed, cut into small cubes and fried in
4–6 tablespoons oil and butter, mixed (for croûtons) – optional

Method
Melt 2 tablespoons of the butter in a large saucepan and add the carrot, onion and bouquet garni. Cover and cook over low heat until the vegetables are tender.

In a pan poach the shrimps in wine for 3–5 minutes or until tender. Strain the shrimps and peel them; if you like, reserve 3 for garnish. Add wine to the vegetables.

Crush the shrimp shells with 4 tablespoons butter or work in a blender with the butter and squeeze through cheesecloth to extract the shrimp butter; reserve it. Finely chop the shrimps and add to vegetable mirepoix.

In a pan melt the remaining butter, stir in the flour and cook, stirring, until pale straw-colored. Cool slightly, pour on the stock and bring to a boil, stirring; season, simmer 2 minutes and add to the shrimp and vegetable mixture. Stir to mix thoroughly and simmer 20 minutes. Work through a tammy strainer or through a regular sieve, then work in a blender so the soup has as smooth a consistency as possible.

Just before serving, bring soup to a boil, add cream and brandy, sherry or Madeira and simmer 2 minutes. Take from heat, stir in shrimp butter piece by piece and taste for seasoning; keep hot, if necessary, in a water bath.
Watchpoint: do not allow soup to boil once cream has been added or it will curdle.

Garnish each bowl of soup with a few croûtons or the reserved shrimps, chopped.

Note: the recipes in this menu serve 10 people.

Garnish each bowl of shrimp bisque with a few croûtons or some chopped shrimps, if you like

Roast Saddle of Lamb Jardinière

2 saddles of lamb (5–6 lb each)
6 tablespoons butter, softened
black pepper, freshly ground
1 cup white wine
$\frac{3}{4}$–1 cup brown stock

For gravy
2 teaspoons flour
2 cups brown stock

Method

Set oven at moderately hot (375°F).

Spread butter over both pieces of lamb and season with pepper. Place them in a large roasting pan, pour over white wine and $\frac{3}{4}$ cup stock and roast in the heated oven, basting every 15–20 minutes and adding more stock if the pan gets dry. Allow $1\frac{1}{2}$–$1\frac{3}{4}$ hours for medium done meat (160°F) on a meat thermometer) or $1\frac{3}{4}$–2 hours for well done meat (175°F on a meat thermometer).

When done, remove saddles of lamb from the pan and let stand 15 minutes in a warm place before carving and arranging on warm platters.

To make gravy: discard the fat from the pan juices, stir in flour and cook to a rich brown color. Stir in the 2 cups brown stock, bring to a boil, stir to dissolve sediment, then simmer until the gravy is well reduced and has a rich flavor. Strain into a sauce boat.

Serve with roast potatoes and a jardinière platter.

How to Càrve a Saddle of Lamb

Set the saddle on a carving platter with the tail end towards you. Run the knife down one side of the backbone and cut under meat that lies on the side of it.

Repeat this on the other side of the bone. Carve wedge-shaped slices down the whole length of each side of backbone, cutting pieces in half if saddle is large.

Cut slanting slices from the tail end of the saddle.

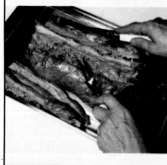

Jardinière Platter

$\frac{3}{4}$ lb carrots
$\frac{3}{4}$ lb Brussels sprouts, trimmed
15–20 small white onions, peeled, or $\frac{3}{4}$ lb zucchini
2 cups ($\frac{1}{2}$ lb) small mushrooms
1 cauliflower
1 tablespoon sugar
salt and pepper
$\frac{1}{2}$ cup butter
1 teaspoon chopped mint
juice of $\frac{1}{2}$ lemon
2 teaspoons chopped parsley

The vegetables on a jardinière platter are all cooked separately and then arranged together for serving.

Method

Carrots: peel and cut in sticks. Cover with cold water, add 1 teaspoon sugar, a pinch of salt, 1 tablespoon butter and cook until carrots are tender; remove the lid and boil until all water has evaporated. Just before serving, reheat gently and stir in 1 teaspoon chopped mint.

Brussels sprouts: cook in boiling salted water for 7–8 minutes or until just tender; drain, refresh and drain again. Just before serving, reheat with $\frac{1}{2}$ tablespoon butter.

Small white onions: blanch by covering with cold water, bringing to a boil and draining well. Return onions to the pan with 2 tablespoons butter and 2 teaspoons sugar; cover and cook slowly for 8–10 minutes or until tender and brown and sticky with caramel. Shake the pan from time to time during cooking to turn the onions. Just before serving, reheat gently.

Zucchini: wash and slice thickly. Blanch in boiling water for 1 minute, drain and return them to the pan with 1 tablespoon butter. Cover pan tightly and cook for 5 minutes. Just before serving, reheat zucchini and cook 2–3 minutes longer or until just tender.

Small mushrooms: wipe with a damp cloth, trim stems level with caps and put in a well-buttered baking dish or saucepan. Season and add a good squeeze of lemon juice. Cover with buttered foil and a lid and bake in hot oven (400°F) with the meat for about 10 minutes or cook in a saucepan on top of the stove for 4–5 minutes or until just tender. Reheat just before serving.

Cauliflower: separate into flowerets and, with a vegetable peeler, peel off any hard outside skin on the little stems. Cook in boiling salted water for about 15 minutes or until just tender. Drain well. Just before serving, reheat in 1 tablespoon butter.

To serve: arrange vegetables in rows on a large hot platter. Melt the remaining butter in a small pan and cook slowly to a nut-brown (noisette). Add lemon juice, salt and pepper and chopped parsley. Pour this butter, while foaming, over the vegetables, particularly the zucchini and cauliflower.

The epitome of elegance

Jardinière platter includes Brussels sprouts, cauliflower, zucchini, carrots and onions

Pineapple en surprise is decorated with spun sugar and served with petits fours — columbines (white fondant icing), suédoises (chocolate fondant icing) and minerves

Dessert

Pineapple en Surprise with Spun Sugar

For pineapple
1 large or 2 medium
   pineapples
4–6 tablespoons sugar
3–4 tablespoons kirsch
1½ quarts orange sherbet
   (see recipe in Volume 11)

For spun sugar
6 tablespoons sugar
6 tablespoons water
pinch of cream of tartar

*Oiled rolling pin or oiled handle
   of a large wooden spoon;
   2 forks*

Method

Cut top off the pineapple and a small slice from the bottom so it stands firmly. With a serrated-edge knife cut out the pineapple flesh in one piece. Cut it into thin slices and cut out the core with an apple corer. Sprinkle the slices with sugar and moisten them with kirsch, cover and refrigerate until ready to serve. Wrap pineapple shell and top in foil or plastic wrap and chill also. Prepare second pineapple as above, if used.

Make orange sherbet and store in freezer.

Not more than 2 hours before serving, make the spun sugar and leave in a cool, dry place.

To serve: set the pineapple shell on a chilled serving dish, fill it with scoops of orange sherbet and replace the top. Surround the shell with the slices of pineapple and decorate them with spun sugar. Serve with an assortment of petits fours.

Accompaniment to dessert

Petits Fours
Basic Foundation

For almond and meringue
   mixture
4 egg whites
¾ cup whole blanched almonds,
   ground
½ cup sugar
5 tablespoons flour

For butter cream
¾ cup quantity butter cream
   frosting 1 (see page 53)
1–2 teaspoons kirsch
½ square (½ oz) semisweet
   chocolate, melted and
   cooled but still soft
1 tablespoon browned, finely
   ground hazelnuts

For fondant icing
2 cup quantity fondant icing
   (see page 52)
1–2 teaspoons dry instant
   coffee
1 teaspoon kirsch
½ square (½ oz) semisweet
   chocolate
sugar syrup (made with ¼ cup
   sugar and ¼ cup water)

To finish
2–3 candied cherries, chopped
few pistachios, halved
few whole hazelnuts

*Pastry bag; ¼ inch plain tube;
   medium star tube*

Makes 30–32 petits fours.

Method

Set oven at moderately hot (375°F) and grease and flour a baking sheet.

Beat egg whites until they hold a stiff peak. Work the almonds, sugar and flour together through a coarse sieve and fold into the egg whites with a large metal spoon.

Put this macaroon mixture into a pastry bag fitted with the plain tube and on the prepared baking sheet pipe one-third in rounds; pipe a second third in ovals and pipe the remainder into small 1½ inch lengths.

Bake the macaroons in the heated oven for 7–8 minutes or until very lightly browned; transfer to a wire rack to cool.

Make butter cream frosting and fondant icing and divide each into 3 portions. Flavor and complete the petits fours as follows:

Columbines

Flavor 1 portion of butter cream frosting with kirsch, put it in a pastry bag fitted with the plain tube and pipe the frosting in a pyramid on top of the round macaroons. Place a tiny piece of candied cherry on top of each pyramid and chill at least 2 hours or freeze 20–30 minutes. Soften 1 portion of fondant icing with some of the sugar syrup, so it is the consistency to coat the back of a spoon thinly, flavor it with kirsch and coat the petits fours — the icing should be thin enough for the cherry to show through.

Suédoises

Flavor a second portion of butter cream frosting with the melted chocolate, put it in a pastry bag fitted with the medium star tube and pipe the frosting along the top of the long macaroons. Chill at least 2 hours or freeze 20–30 minutes. Soften another portion of fondant icing so it is the consistency to coat the back of a spoon, flavor with melted chocolate and coat the petits fours; top each with half a pistachio.

Minerves

Flavor the remaining portion of butter cream frosting with ground hazelnuts, put it in a pastry bag fitted with a plain tube and pipe the frosting on top of the oval macaroons, doming it well. Place a whole hazelnut on top of each one, pushing the nuts down into the cream. Chill at least 2 hours or freeze 20–30 minutes. Soften the remaining portion of fondant icing so it is the consistency to coat the back of a spoon, flavor it with dry instant coffee and coat the petits fours.

To make spun sugar, hold two forks, back to back, and dip the tips of the prongs into the sugar syrup. With a loose wrist movement, flip the forks back and forth until fine threads are thrown

As the forks are moved back and forth, fine threads of spun sugar are thrown over the rolling pin. Remember to cover the floor with paper

Spun Sugar

Working with spun sugar is an art but a simple version is quite easy to make. Spun sugar is very fragile and the threads gradually dissolve on standing. However, it can be kept 1–2 hours in a cool dry atmosphere.

Heat sugar and water in a small pan over low heat until sugar dissolves, then add cream of tartar, dissolved in 1 teaspoon water. Boil rapidly, brushing the sides of the pan occasionally with cold water

to absorb the sugar crystals. When the syrup reaches the extra hard crack stage and forms a brittle thread when dropped in cold water (300°F on a sugar thermometer), dip the bottom of the pan in cold water to stop the boiling. Set aside for 2–3 minutes.

Cover floor with 2–3 sheets of newspaper; have an oiled rolling pin, wooden spoon, or even a clean broom handle ready. If using a wooden spoon or broom handle, put the bowl end or brush end under a board or weight on a

table so the oiled handle extends over the paper-covered floor.

Stand the pan of syrup on a cloth to keep it steady, hold the 2 forks back to back and dip (do not stir) the tips of the prongs into the syrup. Then, with a loose wrist movement flip the forks back and forth over the rolling pin (held in one hand), or over the spoon or broom handle. As you move the forks back and forth you throw fine threads of sugar over the wooden pin or handle.
Watchpoint: let the syrup

stand for about 1 minute before starting to spin it and only dip the tips of the fork prongs into the syrup. If syrup is too thin or there is too much on forks, there will be drops among the threads.

When you have enough threads on the rolling pin or spoon or broom handle, carefully remove them to a convenient storage place. When ready to use, carefully lift sugar threads, fold them very lightly and place them over the dessert that is to be decorated.

Make spun sugar to decorate the pineapple

For chicken Kiev, suprêmes are stuffed with herb butter and deep fried so the butter is trapped inside the crisply coated chicken

FRENCH HAUTE CUISINE

French haute cuisine sets the standard by which all other Western-style cooking is judged. Many other nations produce superb food, but few go to such lengths as the French, who are willing to take infinite care to find just the right ingredients and then spend days preparing a single dish to achieve a perfect balance of flavor and texture, complemented by just the right garnish. The sauces are particularly famous — rich, subtle and superbly smooth, they range from creamy, delicate sauce suprême, flavored with veal, fish or chicken stock, to the limitless variations of brown sauce, served with rich meats and game.

Not all the dishes in this feature on haute cuisine involve long, complicated preparation but they do have some special ingredient like truffles or call for a skill that makes them a luxury to be reserved for special occasions.

Oeufs Richelieu
(Eggs Richelieu)

8 fresh eggs
4 cups cool but still liquid
   aspic, made with chicken or
   veal stock
1 canned truffle, drained and
   sliced, or 4 small cooked,
   peeled shrimps (for
   decoration)
bunch of watercress (optional)

For shrimp mousse
$\frac{3}{4}$ lb cooked, peeled shrimps
$\frac{1}{3}$ cup unsalted butter,
   softened
thick béchamel sauce, made
   with 2 tablespoons butter,
   2 tablespoons flour, 1 cup
   milk (infused with slice of
   onion, 6 peppercorns, blade
   of mace and bay leaf)
2–3 tablespoons heavy cream
salt and pepper

For chaudfroid sauce
béchamel sauce, made with
   2 tablespoons butter,
   2 tablespoons flour, 2 cups
   milk (infused with slice of
   onion, 6 peppercorns, blade
   of mace and bay leaf)
3 tablespoons heavy cream
salt and pepper
$\frac{1}{2}$ cup cool but still liquid
   aspic, made with veal or
   chicken stock
1 envelope gelatin

This classic buffet dish consists of poached eggs, coated with a white chaudfroid sauce and decorated with truffles or shrimps, then set on a shrimp mousse and garnished with chopped aspic.

Method

Poach the eggs until just firm to the touch, taking care to keep them plump and round; keep them in cold water.

To make the shrimp mousse: work the shrimps twice through the fine blade of a grinder. Pound them in a mortar and pestle or work in a blender until smooth, then gradually work in the softened butter. Stir in the béchamel sauce; fold in the cream and season carefully; the mousse should be light in consistency and should just drop from the spoon. Chill it.

Make the chaudfroid sauce (see page 92).

Lift the eggs from the water with a slotted spoon, gently pat dry with paper towels and set on a wire rack over a tray. Set the chaudfroid sauce over a bowl of ice water and stir until it starts to set. Spoon the sauce over the eggs and chill until it is set; add another coating of sauce and chill well. Decorate with sliced truffle or a shrimp half and coat with aspic on the point of setting. Chill until firm.

To finish, spoon a $\frac{1}{4}$ inch layer of aspic into an oval silver or stainless steel platter and chill until set. Pour the remaining aspic into a cake pan, chill until set, then chop it. Spoon the shrimp mousse down the center of the platter, smooth it, then set the eggs carefully on top. Garnish the sides with chopped aspic and watercress, if you like.

Quenelles Nantua

$\frac{1}{2}$ lb salmon steak
salmon mousseline (made with
   $1\frac{1}{4}$ lb salmon steaks or fillets,
   3 egg whites, 1 cup heavy
   cream, salt and pepper)
2 cups Nantua sauce
8 bouchée cases, made with
   $1\frac{1}{2}$ cup quantity puff pastry
   (see Volume 8)
$\frac{1}{2}$ cup water
squeeze of lemon juice
1 cup ($\frac{1}{4}$ lb) mushrooms, sliced
1 tablespoon butter
8 small cooked, peeled shrimps
   (for garnish)

Nantua is the name given to dishes that include a shrimp (or crayfish) garnish or purée.

Method

To make salmon mousseline: wash and dry the fish and remove any bones. Pass twice through the fine blade of a grinder, then pound until smooth in a mortar and pestle and gradually work in the egg whites. Or instead of pounding, work the ground fish with egg whites for a few seconds in a blender until very smooth. Gradually beat in cream and add seasonings. Chill well.

Wash and dry the salmon steak, place in a baking dish with the water and lemon juice, cover with buttered foil and poach in a moderate oven (350°F) for 15–20 minutes or until the fish flakes easily. Drain the fish on paper towels and flake it, discarding the skin and bones. Sauté mushrooms in butter until tender and add to the salmon.

To make the quenelles: bring a large pan of salted water to a boil. Put the mousseline into the quenelle molds and lower them into the water, or shape the mixture into ovals with 2 soup spoons and lower them gently into the water. At once reduce the heat so the water is barely simmering and poach the quenelles for 10–12 minutes or until they are firm to the touch. Drain them carefully on paper towels, arrange them in a serving dish and keep warm.

Mix enough Nantua sauce with the salmon and mushrooms to bind the mixture, heat gently until very warm and put into the bouchées. Top each one with a cooked shrimp. Coat quenelles with the remaining sauce and arrange bouchées around the edge of the dish.

Nantua Sauce

$1\frac{1}{2}$ tablespoons butter
$1\frac{1}{2}$ tablespoons flour
$1\frac{1}{2}$ cups well-flavored fish
   stock (made with 1 onion,
   $\frac{1}{2}$ tablespoon butter, $\frac{1}{2}$ lb
   fish bones, 1 small carrot,
   $\frac{1}{2}$ stalk of celery, bouquet
   garni, 3 peppercorns, $\frac{1}{4}$ cup
   white wine, slice of lemon,
   $1\frac{1}{2}$ cups water)
$\frac{1}{2}$ cup heavy cream
salt and pepper
small can truffle pieces,
   drained and chopped
few drops of pink food coloring

For shrimp butter
$\frac{1}{4}$ lb uncooked, unpeeled
   shrimps
$\frac{1}{4}$ cup butter

Makes 2 cups.

Method

To make shrimp butter: finely chop the shrimps, then pound them with their shells in a mortar and pestle; beat in the butter. Alternatively, work shrimps and their shells with the butter in a blender. Let stand 10–15 minutes. Work through a fine strainer or squeeze in cheesecloth to extract shrimp butter.

To make Nantua sauce: melt the $1\frac{1}{2}$ tablespoons butter, stir in the flour off the heat and pour in fish stock. Bring to a boil, stirring, and simmer 3–5 minutes or until the sauce is the consistency of heavy cream. Add the cream, take from the heat and cool a little. Beat in shrimp butter a little at a time, add the truffles and pink food coloring to tint the sauce a delicate pink; taste for seasoning.
Watchpoint: do not allow sauce to boil after adding the butter or it will separate.

Quenelles de brochet are coated with Nantua sauce (recipe is on page 22)

Quenelles de Brochet

1½ lb pike, halibut or haddock, free from skin and bone
2 eggs
2 tablespoons butter, creamed
salt and pepper
2 cups mushroom cream sauce or 2 cups Nantua sauce (see page 20)

For panada
¼ cup butter
½ cup water mixed with ½ cup milk
6 tablespoons flour, sifted twice with ¼ teaspoon salt

The firm close texture of pike is ideal for making these famous fish dumplings that should be soft, light and fluffy.

Method

Work fish twice through fine blade of grinder, then measure it – there should be 2 cups.

To make panada: melt butter in water and milk, bring just to a boil, take from heat, and at once add all the flour. Beat well until mixture is smooth and pulls away from the sides of the pan; spread on a plate to cool.

Watchpoint: the volume of panada and fish should now be approximately equal.

Pound fish in a mortar and pestle until smooth, then gradually work in the panada. Transfer to a bowl and beat in the eggs, one at a time, beating well between each addition. Beat in the creamed butter with seasoning, cover tightly and chill overnight.

Watchpoint: after adding the eggs, the mixture will be quite soft, but will stiffen in the refrigerator.

To cook quenelles: shape mixture into ovals, using 2 soup spoons, or roll it lightly to 3-inch cork shapes. Bring a shallow pan of salted water to a boil, carefully lower in the quenelles and simmer, uncovered for 18–20 minutes or until firm to the touch. Lift them out with a slotted spoon, touch the bowl of the spoon on a paper towel to remove any moisture and place the quenelles in a buttered gratin dish or shallow baking dish.

Coat the quenelles with mushroom cream sauce or Nantua sauce and bake in a moderate oven (350°F) for 5–10 minutes or until the quenelles puff slightly. Serve at once.

Mushroom Cream Sauce

1 cup (¼ lb) mushrooms, thinly sliced
2–3 tablespoons butter
juice of ½ lemon
2 cups velouté sauce, made with 3 tablespoons butter, 2 tablespoons flour, 2¼–2½ cups well-flavored veal or chicken stock and salt and pepper

Method

Cook the mushrooms in the butter and lemon juice for 1–2 minutes or until tender.

To make velouté sauce: in a pan melt the butter, stir in the flour and cook until it is pale straw-colored. Take from the heat, cool a little and pour in the stock. Bring to a boil, stirring, and simmer until the sauce is glossy and coats the back of a spoon. Add the mushrooms and taste for seasoning.

Mousse de Saumon à la Nantua
(Salmon Mousse Nantua)

1 cup (½ lb) cooked fresh salmon, flaked and free from skin and bone
béchamel sauce, made with 2 tablespoons butter, 2 tablespoons flour, 1½ cups milk (infused with slice of onion, 6 peppercorns, blade of mace and bay leaf)
¾ cup mayonnaise
salt and pepper
1 envelope gelatin
¼ cup chicken stock or water
½ cup heavy cream, whipped until it holds a soft shape
6–8 cooked, peeled medium shrimps, coarsely chopped

For garnish
5–6 tablespoons mayonnaise
2–3 tablespoons tomato juice
dash of Tabasco
1 hard-cooked egg
bunch of watercress
few shrimps (optional)

Soufflé dish or cake pan (1½ quart capacity)

Method

Lightly oil the dish or pan.

Pound the salmon in a mortar and pestle until smooth and beat in the béchamel sauce; alternatively, purée the salmon with a little of the sauce in a blender. Add remaining sauce and mayonnaise and season well. Sprinkle the gelatin over the stock or water in a small pan and let stand 5 minutes until spongy. Dissolve over a pan of hot water and stir into salmon mixture with the chopped shrimps. Chill in refrigerator or over pan of ice water, stirring occasionally, until on the point of setting, then fold in the cream and adjust seasoning. Pour the mixture into prepared dish or pan, cover and chill at least 2 hours until set.

A short time before serving unmold the mousse onto a platter.

To prepare garnish: thin the mayonnaise to coating consistency with tomato juice, add Tabasco to taste and spoon over mousse. Halve the egg and shred white. Work the yolk through a sieve onto the mousse. Decorate the edge with shredded egg white, watercress and extra shrimps, if you like.

Truite en Gelée
(Trout in Aspic)

4 whole trout ($\frac{3}{4}$–1 lb each)
1 cup white wine or wine and water mixed (for poaching)
salt and pepper

For fish aspic
2$\frac{1}{2}$ cups strong fish stock
1 cup liquid (from cooking fish)
2 envelopes gelatin
$\frac{1}{2}$ cup sherry
$\frac{1}{2}$ cup white wine
2 egg whites

For garnish
8 medium tomatoes, peeled
$\frac{1}{4}$ cup mayonnaise
$\frac{1}{4}$ lb cooked, peeled shrimps
1$\frac{1}{2}$ lb asparagus, cooked and cooled (see page 87)
1$\frac{1}{2}$ cups green mayonnaise (for serving) – optional

Method
Set the oven at moderately low (325°F).

Trim, wash and dry the trout, leaving heads on, and lay them in a baking dish. Pour over the white wine or wine and water, season lightly, cover and poach in heated oven for 20–25 minutes or until eyes of fish turn white. Let trout cool to tepid in the liquid, then lift them out and peel off skin, leaving head and tail intact. Set the trout on a wire rack over a tray and chill.

Strain the cooking liquid, measure 1 cup and add to the fish stock. Make the aspic and let cool.

To prepare the garnish: cut tops from the peeled tomatoes at the rounded (not stem) end and scoop out the seeds. Mix the mayonnaise with the chopped shrimps, fill tomatoes with the mixture, mounding it up well and replace tomato tops on a slant. Divide cooked asparagus into 4 or 6 small piles. Chill the asparagus and tomatoes.

When the aspic is on the point of setting, spoon or brush it over the trout to coat them. Chill until set, then add another coating of aspic, if necessary. Coat the asparagus also with aspic and chill. Pour a $\frac{1}{4}$ inch layer of aspic into a silver or stainless steel platter and chill until set.

Arrange the trout diagonally down the center of the platter, surround with the piles of glazed asparagus and add another coating of aspic, if you like. Place the stuffed tomatoes between the asparagus piles and serve the green mayonnaise separately, if you like.

Green Mayonnaise

Into 1$\frac{1}{2}$ cups mayonnaise stir 2 tablespoons finely chopped parsley, 1 tablespoon finely chopped chives, 1 tablespoon finely chopped tarragon and 1 teaspoon finely chopped dill. Alternatively, purée herbs with the mayonnaise in a blender. Cover the mayonnaise and let stand in a cool place at least 2 hours for the flavor to mellow before serving.

Suprêmes de Poisson Parisienne
(Fish Molds with Mushrooms)

For fish mousseline
1 lb halibut, haddock or other firm white fish, free from skin and bone
2 egg whites, beaten until broken up
1 cup heavy cream
salt and pepper

For salpicon
1 cup ($\frac{1}{4}$ lb) mushrooms, thinly sliced
1 tablespoon butter
1 tablespoon fish stock or sherry

For suprême sauce
velouté sauce (made with 1$\frac{1}{2}$ tablespoons butter, 1$\frac{1}{2}$ tablespoons flour, 1 cup well-flavored fish stock, salt and pepper)
2 egg yolks
$\frac{1}{2}$ cup heavy cream

For garnish
2 cups ($\frac{1}{2}$ lb) small mushrooms, trimmed and sautéed in 2 tablespoons butter

8 deep tartlet pans

Method
Butter the tartlet pans.

To make the mousseline: work the fish twice through the fine blade of a grinder and measure it — there should be 1$\frac{1}{2}$ cups. Pound the mixture in a mortar and pestle until smooth and gradually work in the egg whites. Or, instead of pounding, work the ground fish with the egg white for a few seconds in a blender until very smooth. Gradually beat in the cream, then add seasoning.

Watchpoint: if the kitchen is hot, put the mixture in a metal bowl over a bowl of ice to chill it thoroughly while working in the cream. Do not season the mousseline until egg whites and cream have been worked in — the consistency should be like whipped cream. If the mousseline is at all soft, a pinch of salt will stiffen it at once.

To make salpicon: sauté the sliced mushrooms quickly in the butter until soft, add the fish stock or sherry and season.

Fill the prepared pans almost full with the mousseline. Dip your finger or the bowl of a teaspoon into a little egg white and hollow out the center of each mold. Fill the mushroom salpicon into the hollows, then cover completely with the mousseline mixture. Level the tops with a knife.

Bring a shallow pan of salted water to a boil and lower in the pans so they are completely covered. Poach them 8–10 minutes, shaking the pan handle once or twice during cooking; the suprêmes will detach themselves from the molds and float to the surface when they are cooked.

Meanwhile make the suprême sauce and add the liaison of egg yolks and cream.

When the suprêmes are cooked, lift them out carefully with a slotted spatula and drain on paper towels.

To serve, arrange the suprêmes on a platter, spoon over the suprême sauce, garnish with sautéed mushrooms, and serve at once.

Note: dariole molds or custard cups can be used instead of tartlet pans but the suprêmes must then be poached in a water bath in a moderate oven (350°F). They should be cooked for 20–25 minutes or until firm to the touch.

Lobster Bordelaise – the recipe was created at the famous Chapon Fin restaurant in Bordeaux

Lobster Bordelaise

4 live lobsters (1–1¼ lb each)
6 tablespoons butter
¼ cup brandy
1 bottle dry white Bordeaux
  wine
salt and pepper
8 egg yolks (for liaison)
½ cup heavy cream
  (for liaison)
pinch of cayenne
1 tablespoon chopped parsley
bunch of watercress (for
  garnish)

For mirepoix
3 tablespoons butter
2 carrots, finely diced
2 onions, finely diced
2 stalks of celery, finely diced
¼ teaspoon thyme
1 bay leaf

This recipe was created in the 1930's at the famous Chapon Fin restaurant in Bordeaux.

Method

For the mirepoix: in a skillet melt the butter, add the vegetables, herbs and seasoning, cover and cook gently, stirring occasionally, until the vegetables are very tender.

To kill live lobsters with a knife: lay each one in turn flat on a board, hard shell up, with the head facing to the right, tail to the left; cover the tail with a cloth. Hold the lobster firmly behind the head with your left hand and with the point of a sharp knife, pierce down to the board through the cross mark that lies on the center of the head. The lobster is killed at once. Continue splitting the lobster body in half. Repeat with the other lobsters.

Discard the head sacs and scoop out the soft meat and any coral from the bodies of the lobsters and reserve.

In a roasting pan melt ¼ cup of the butter, add the lobsters cut sides down, and cook gently for 5 minutes. Add the brandy and flame. Add the mirepoix, white wine and seasoning and bring almost to a boil. Cook in a moderate oven (350°F) for 10–15 minutes or until the lobsters are bright red.

Take out the lobsters, remove meat from claws, legs and tail. Slice it and replace in the shell. Arrange on a hot platter. Strain the cooking liquid into a saucepan and boil until reduced to about 2½ cups. Mix the egg yolks with the heavy cream, body meat and any coral from the lobsters. Stir in a little of the hot liquid, and stir this liaison back into the remaining hot liquid. Heat very gently, stirring constantly, until the sauce thickens.

Watchpoint: do not let it become too hot or it will curdle.

Take the sauce from the heat and beat in the remaining 2 tablespoons butter, a piece at a time. Do not reheat or it will separate.

Add a pinch of cayenne and taste for seasoning. Spoon the sauce over the lobsters and reheat for 2 minutes in a hot oven or for ½ minute under the broiler. Sprinkle with parsley just before serving and garnish the platter with watercress.

Poussins Farcis en Gelée
(Stuffed Small Chickens in Aspic)

2 broiling chickens (2–2½ lb each)

For stuffing
2 shallots or scallions, finely chopped
1 tablespoon butter
¾ lb ground veal or pork
2 teaspoons chopped parsley
½ teaspoon thyme
1 cup fresh white breadcrumbs
salt and pepper
1 egg, beaten to mix

For roasting
¼ cup butter
1 cup stock, made from chicken giblets

For garnish
2 cups cool but still liquid aspic, made with chicken stock
bunch of watercress

For salad
1 ripe honeydew or Crenshaw melon
2 cucumbers, peeled, seeded and cut in 1½ inch sticks
⅓ cup vinaigrette dressing, made with lemon juice

Trussing needle and string

Method

Bone the chickens (see Volume 1), leaving the wing bones in; set the oven at hot (400°F).

To make the stuffing: fry the shallots or scallions in the butter until soft but not brown. Cool, add to the ground veal or pork with herbs and breadcrumbs and mix well with plenty of seasoning. Add enough beaten egg to bind the mixture.

Lay the chickens, cut side up, on a board, season the cut surfaces and spread with stuffing. Sew up the birds with a trussing needle and string and truss them so they sit up well and hold their shape.

Set the chickens in a large roasting pan, spread the breasts with butter and pour around ½ cup stock. Cover with buttered foil, tucking it down loosely, and roast in the heated oven for about 1 hour or until a meat thermometer inserted in the center registers 170°F, or a skewer inserted in the center for 1 minute is hot to the touch when withdrawn. Baste the chickens often during cooking and turn them from one side to the other, then onto their backs, so they brown evenly. Let cool, then chill them.

Add the remaining stock to the pan and boil, stirring to dissolve the juices. Chill the juices, then discard the fat that solidifies on top and add the juices to the stock for making aspic. Make aspic and cool it.

Cut chickens carefully in half, discarding the trussing strings. Arrange the birds, overlapping, down the center of a large silver or stainless steel platter and chill. When the aspic is on the point of setting, spoon it over the chickens to coat them, chill until set, then add another coating of aspic. Chill again until firmly set.

To make the salad, sprinkle the cucumber with salt, cover and let stand 30 minutes to draw out the juices (dégorger). Rinse and dry on paper towels. Scoop the melon flesh from the shells with a ball cutter, add to the cucumber and toss with vinaigrette dressing. Spoon the salad down one side of the platter and garnish with watercress.

Poulet à la Kiev
(Chicken Kiev)

4 suprêmes of chicken
½ cup butter
grated rind and juice of 1 lemon
salt
black pepper, freshly ground
pinch of ground mace or
    nutmeg
2 teaspoons chopped parsley
½ teaspoon tarragon
½ teaspoon chives

For coating
¼ cup seasoned flour (made
    with ¼ teaspoon salt, pinch
    of pepper)
1 egg, beaten to mix
¾ cup dry white breadcrumbs
deep fat (for frying)

Chop frills (see box)

This dish is basically simple but it must be carefully prepared. The chicken breasts are stuffed with herb butter and fried in deep fat so that the melted butter is trapped inside the crisply coated chicken — warn your guests that the butter may spurt out when the chicken is pierced.

Method
Cream the butter and beat in the lemon rind and juice, seasoning, mace or nutmeg and herbs. Form into a 2½ inch square cake on a sheet of wax paper, cover and chill until very firm.
Lay the chicken suprêmes between 2 sheets of wax paper and beat them with a mallet or rolling pin to three-eighth inch thickness.
Note: boned chicken breasts can be used instead of the suprêmes.
Cut the chilled herb butter into 4 sticks, set a stick of butter on each suprême, fold over the end furthest from the wing bone and roll up so the butter is completely enclosed

and the wing bone protrudes at the other end. Roll in seasoned flour, brush with beaten egg and coat with dry breadcrumbs, pressing them in well with a spatula. Chill, uncovered, at least 3–4 hours, so the coating can dry.
The suprêmes may also be tightly wrapped and frozen; let them thaw in the refrigerator for 6–7 hours before frying.
To fry suprêmes: heat the fat to 375°F on a fat thermometer and lower them carefully into the hot, deep fat. Fry them until golden brown — this should take at least 4 minutes so that the suprêmes are thoroughly cooked. Drain on paper towels, set a chop frill on each bone and serve very hot.

For chicken Kiev, wrap suprême around herb butter

Poulet Xenia
(Chicken Xenia)

Follow the recipe for chicken Kiev but instead of herb butter use pieces of pâté de foie gras, preferably with some pieces of truffle.

The origin of **chicken Kiev** is obscure. The dish is well known in Russia but it is mentioned in few classic French cookbooks, though the recipe is typically French. It was probably created by one of the French chefs often employed by noble Russian families at the turn of the last century.

A **suprême** is all the white meat on the breast down to the wing bone on a chicken. It should be removed in one piece from the bones on each side.
To cut a suprême, cut down from the top of the breastbone with a sharp knife, taking care to keep the knife close to rib cage, and detach all the white meat in one piece with the wing bone attached.

To Make Chop Frills

Fold a 10 X 3 inch sheet of plain white paper in half lengthwise. With scissors make a series of even cuts one-eighth inch apart to within ¾ inch of the unfolded long edges and turn the paper inside out so the cut part is looped. Stick the two long edges together with glue and cut to make 4 frills. Fold each in a circle and attach the ends to complete the chop frill.

Mousse de Poulet Madrilène
(Chicken Mousse Madrilène)

3½–4 lb roasting chicken or fowl
1 carrot, sliced
1 onion, sliced
bouquet garni
6 peppercorns
salt and pepper

For mousse
béchamel sauce, made with
    2 tablespoons butter,
    2 tablespoons flour, 1½ cups
    milk (infused with slice of
    onion, 6 peppercorns, blade
    of mace and bay leaf)
½ cup unsalted butter,
    softened
2 tablespoons sherry
1 cup heavy cream, whipped
    until it holds a soft shape
4 cups aspic, made with stock
    from cooking the chicken
3–4 slices of cooked ham
    (⅓ lb), cut in strips
3–4 slices of cooked tongue
    (⅓ lb), cut in strips
3 medium tomatoes, peeled
    and sliced

Clear glass bowl or straight-sided glass dish (2 quart capacity)

Method
Put the chicken in a kettle with carrot, onion, bouquet garni, peppercorns, a little salt and enough water to reach the top of the thigh bones; if using a fowl, cover it completely with water. Cover the pan, bring to a boil and simmer for about 1 hour for chicken, or 1¼ hours for fowl, or until no pink juice runs out when the thigh is pierced with a skewer. Let cool in the liquid, then take out the bird and strain the cooking liquid. Use 4 cups of this liquid to make aspic and let cool.
To make the mousse: re-

move chicken meat, discarding the bones and skin, and work the meat twice through the fine blade of a grinder. Make the béchamel sauce and let cool.

Pound the chicken in a mortar and pestle until smooth, then work in the cool béchamel sauce. Or instead of pounding, work ground chicken meat with the sauce in a blender. Beat in the softened butter with the sherry and seasoning. Stir in the lightly whipped cream and taste for seasoning.

Spread about one-third of chicken mousse in the bottom of the bowl or dish and smooth the top. Spoon $\frac{1}{4}$ cup cool but still liquid aspic carefully on top and chill until set. Mix the ham and tongue strips and spread half on top of the aspic. Add $\frac{1}{4}$–$\frac{1}{2}$ cup more liquid aspic just to cover the ham and tongue; chill until set. Add a layer of half the remaining chicken mousse with a little aspic on top, chill and continue adding layers of ham and tongue, aspic and chicken, until all are used, finishing with chicken.

Smooth top of the mousse, coat with a thin layer of aspic and chill until set. Arrange the tomatoes, overlapping slightly, on top, and fill with remaining aspic. Chill 2 hours or until firmly set before serving.

Poulade Truffée
(Chicken with Truffles)

3$\frac{1}{2}$–4 lb plump roasting chicken
1 small can truffles
sprig of thyme or $\frac{1}{4}$ teaspoon
   dried thyme
small bay leaf
salt and pepper
1–2 thin slices of fresh pork
   fat (for barding)
2 tablespoons brandy
$\frac{1}{4}$ cup Madeira

Trussing needle and string

Method
Set oven at moderate (350°F).
Drain the truffles, reserving the liquid, trim them to neat ovals and cut in thin slices; chop the trimmings and add to the liquid.

Lift the skin of the chicken breast and carefully insert your fingers to detach the skin, without breaking it, from the meat. Insert the slices of truffle between skin and breast meat in a neat pattern on each side of the bird. Put the thyme and bay leaf inside the bird, season the inside and truss it. Wrap the chicken in the pork fat, tying it in place, then wrap in foil. Set in a roasting pan and bake in heated oven for 1$\frac{1}{2}$–1$\frac{3}{4}$ hours or until no pink juice runs out when the thigh is pierced with a skewer. Ten minutes before the end of cooking, remove the foil and pork fat, baste the bird well with the liquid in the foil and cook 10 minutes longer or until the bird is very lightly browned but the truffles can still be seen clearly.

Take out the chicken, trim the wing pinions, set on a platter and keep warm. Discard any fat from roasting pan, add brandy and Madeira, bring to a boil and strain into a saucepan. Add the reserved truffle trimmings and liquid,

simmer 1 minute and taste for seasoning. Spoon this gravy over the chicken and serve with boiled rice or rice pilaf.

Pheasant
Viroflay

1 large young pheasant or
   2 young hen pheasants
$\frac{1}{4}$ cup butter
1 dessert apple, cored and
   sliced
$\frac{3}{4}$ cup stock
$\frac{1}{2}$ cup white wine or $\frac{1}{4}$ cup
   sherry
2 tablespoons heavy cream

For stuffing
$\frac{1}{2}$ lb salt pork
1 shallot, finely chopped
$\frac{1}{4}$ cup butter
1 cup fresh white breadcrumbs
$\frac{1}{2}$ lb leaf spinach, blanched
   and chopped
2 egg yolks
$\frac{1}{2}$ teaspoon thyme
$\frac{1}{2}$ teaspoon sage
salt and pepper

Trussing needle and string

This recipe is also delicious when made with chicken.

Method
Set oven at hot (400°F).
Bone pheasant as for chicken (see Volume 1), but leave in the leg and wing bones.

To prepare stuffing: cook salt pork in boiling water for 30 minutes, drain and grind. Cook the shallot in butter until soft but not brown and mix with all the other stuffing ingredients; season well.

Fill the bird or birds with the stuffing, sew up with string and truss neatly. Rub the bird with the butter and place in a roasting pan with the apple slices and stock. Roast in heated oven for about

45 minutes, basting and turning the bird occasionally. Remove pheasant from the pan, discard trussing strings, cut the bird in half or in quarters and arrange on a warm platter. Pour fat from pan and discard. Deglaze the pan juices with the wine or sherry, bring to a boil and strain. Add the cream to this gravy, taste for seasoning and spoon it over the bird. Serve with braised celery.

Stuffed squabs, garnished with peas and carrots, are arranged on a platter with slices of tongue between them

Pigeons Farcis St. Cyr
(Stuffed Squabs with Peas and Carrots)

4 wild pigeons or squabs
3 tablespoons butter
½ cup white wine
1 cup well-flavored veal stock

For stuffing
1 cup (¼ lb) mushrooms, finely
    chopped
squeeze of lemon juice
¼ cup butter
½ lb ground lean veal or pork
2 slices (2 oz) of cooked
    tongue, finely chopped
salt and pepper

For garnish
¼ cup butter
2 cups shelled fresh green
    peas or 1 package frozen
    peas, thawed
heart of Boston lettuce,
    washed and quartered
2 teaspoons sugar
¼ cup water
bunch of small carrots,
    scrubbed and trimmed, or
    6–8 medium carrots, shaped
    into ovals
10–12 small onions, peeled
4 slices of cooked tongue
1 tablespoon Madeira or
    sherry

Trussing needle and string

Method
Set oven at moderate (350°F).

Bone the pigeons or squabs (see Volume 1), discarding ribs and backbones but leaving in leg and wing bones.

To make the stuffing: gently cook mushrooms with a squeeze of lemon juice in the butter for 2–3 minutes; let cool. Mix ground veal or pork with mushrooms, tongue and plenty of seasoning.

Lay the boned birds, cut side up, on a board, sprinkle with salt and pepper and spread with stuffing. Sew up birds with a trussing needle and string to hold their shape, keeping them plump.

Melt the 3 tablespoons butter in a shallow flameproof casserole and brown birds on all sides over low heat. Season lightly, cover pan tightly and bake in heated oven for about 1¼ hours for the pigeons or 45 minutes for the squabs, or until a skewer inserted in the center of the birds for 1 minute is hot to the touch when withdrawn.

To make the garnish: thickly spread a flameproof casserole with 2 tablespoons of butter, add the peas, lettuce heart, salt and pepper, 1 teaspoon sugar and the water. Cover and simmer 15 minutes. Put the carrots in another pan with the remaining butter, sugar and a little salt. Add water to cover, cover pan, bring to a boil and simmer 10–20 minutes (depending on age of the carrots) or until almost tender. Remove the lid and boil rapidly until liquid is reduced to a shiny glaze.

Cook the onions in boiling salted water for 5 minutes, drain them, add to the peas and cook 10 minutes longer or until peas and onions are tender. Cut the tongue slices in half, put them in a pan with the Madeira or sherry and heat very gently.

To serve, take out birds, discard trussing strings and cut birds in half, pressing the stuffing into them. Arrange in a circle on a round platter with a slice of tongue between each half bird. Put peas and onions in the center and pile carrots on top; keep warm.

Discard any fat from the casserole, add the wine, bring to a boil and stir to dissolve pan juices. Add the veal stock, simmer 1–2 minutes and strain. Bring back to a boil, season and spoon over birds.

Bone the birds, discarding the ribs and backbones, but leave in leg and wing bones

Spoon peas and onion mixture into center of the platter, then pile the carrots on top

Cold beef, coated with aspic and decorated with egg and truffle, is served with tomato baskets and artichoke bottoms filled with peas

Filet de Boeuf en Gelée Bouquetière
(Beef Fillet in Aspic with Artichoke and Tomato Baskets)

4 lb beef fillet
2 tablespoons oil

To decorate
4 cups cool, but still liquid,
  aspic, made with beef stock
small can truffles, drained
2 hard-cooked eggs, peeled

For garnish
4 small artichokes
1½ cups fresh peas or 1 package
  frozen peas
1 cucumber, peeled, seeded
  and diced
4 even-sized tomatoes

¾–1 inch plain piping tube

Method
Set the oven at hot (400°F).

To roast beef fillet: heat the oil in a roasting pan, baste the beef and roast in heated oven (400°F) for 1 hour or until a meat thermometer inserted in the center registers 140°F for rare beef. Let the beef stand at room temperature until cool.

Make the aspic and let cool.

To prepare garnish: trim the artichoke stems, cut the tops, leaving about 1 inch of the lower leaves and cook in boiling salted water 20–25 minutes or until tender when pierced with a fork. Drain, scoop out the hairy chokes with a teaspoon and discard them; chill the artichokes.

Cook fresh peas in boiling salted water 10–15 minutes or until just tender, or cook frozen peas according to package directions. Drain, refresh and drain again thoroughly. Pile peas on artichoke

bottoms and chill.

Sprinkle the diced cucumber with salt, cover and let stand 15 minutes to draw out the juices (dégorger). Rinse with cold water. Cut 2 wedges from each side of the tomatoes to form baskets, leaving a slice in the center to make a handle (see Garnishes in Volume 15). Scoop out the seeds with a teaspoon, season, fill the tomatoes with cucumber and chill.

When the beef is cool, cut 6–8 half-inch slices from it and lay them on a wire rack. Set the remaining piece of beef on the rack and chill.

To prepare decoration: cut very thin slices of truffle and hard-cooked egg white. With a small knife cut the truffle into even-sized triangles and cut equal triangles of egg white; with the plain piping tube or a bottle top, cut 6–8 circles of egg white. Put the triangles and circles on a plate and spoon over enough aspic to moisten them.

Set the wire rack with the beef on a tray and spoon over enough cool but still liquid aspic to coat the slices and whole piece of beef. Chill until set, then decorate the slices of beef with circles of egg white topped by a triangle of truffle. Arrange the triangles of egg white and truffle on the whole piece of beef to make a checkerboard pattern and chill until set — the aspic on the pieces of decoration will make them stick to the beef. Coat the beef with aspic again and chill until set.

Pour a ¼ inch layer of liquid aspic onto a silver or stainless steel platter and chill until set. Place the piece of beef and the slices on the platter and arrange the tomato baskets and artichoke bottoms around it. Coat them all with aspic and chill at least 2 hours before serving.

Chateaubriand

1–1¼ lb Chateaubriand beef
  steak
3–4 tablespoons melted butter
  or oil (for basting)
salt
black pepper, freshly ground

For serving
maître d'hôtel butter or
  Béarnaise sauce
château potatoes
bunch of watercress (for
  garnish)

This classic cut, a cross between a steak and a roast, is a very thick slice from the middle of a beef fillet. It is always broiled and must be cooked very carefully so the outside does not burn and harden before the meat is done. Chateaubriand should always be served rare. Serves 2.

Method
Brush the Chateaubriand with melted butter or oil, sprinkle

Classic Chateaubriand, a thick cut from the beef fillet, is served with château potatoes

it with pepper and broil it, preferably over charcoal, for 20–25 minutes. Brush it often with melted butter or oil during cooking and turn it 2–3 times so it browns evenly on all sides. Sprinkle lightly with salt, arrange it on a platter with château potatoes and a bunch of watercress at either end. Top the Chateaubriand with maître d'hôtel butter, or serve Béarnaise sauce separately.

Let the meat stand in a warm place for 10 minutes before carving to let the juices 'set'. Carve in diagonal 1 inch slices, giving each person some of the brown outside and rare inside slices.

Veal en croûte is baked in a puff pastry shell and served with suprême sauce

Rôti de Veau en Croûte
(Veal in Pastry)

2½–3 lb boneless lean veal
    roast, rolled and tied
1 tablespoon oil
2 tablespoons butter
salt and pepper
6–8 savory crêpes
3 cup quantity puff pastry
    (see Volume 8)
1 egg, beaten to mix (for glaze)

For salpicon
1 calf's or lamb's sweetbread
    (¼–⅓ lb)
2 tablespoons butter
1 shallot, finely chopped
1 cup (¼ lb) mushrooms,
    chopped
2–3 slices of lemon or a few
    drops of vinegar

For suprême sauce
1 cup (¼ lb) mushrooms,
    thinly sliced
squeeze of lemon juice
velouté sauce (made with
    1½ tablespoons butter,
    1½ tablespoons flour, 1 cup
    well-flavored veal stock, salt
    and pepper)
2 egg yolks
½ cup heavy cream

The veal roast should be long rather than short and thick in shape.

Method

To prepare the sweetbread: soak for 3–5 hours in cold water with 1–2 slices of lemon or a few drops of vinegar. Rinse, put in a pan of cold water with a little salt and another slice of lemon and bring slowly to a boil over low heat, skimming from time to time. Drain the sweetbread, rinse it in cold water and remove any ducts and skin. Press it between 2 plates with a weight on top for 2 hours or until cold, then cut in ½ inch slices.

Make puff pastry dough and chill.

Set the oven at moderate (350°F).

In a flameproof casserole heat the oil and butter and brown the veal thoroughly on all sides. Sprinkle with seasoning, cover and bake in the heated oven for 1¼ hours. Take out and let cool.

Make the crêpes and keep covered.

To make the salpicon: in a skillet melt the butter and cook the shallot over low heat until soft but not browned. Add the mushrooms and cook 1–2 minutes. Add the sliced sweetbread, season and cook the mixture gently for 4–5 minutes. Spread on a plate to cool.

Roll out the pastry dough to a rectangle 4 inches longer and 6 inches wider than the veal. Lay 2–3 crêpes overlapping down the center of the dough, spread them with half the salpicon and set the veal upside down on top. Top with the remaining salpicon and cover with the remaining crêpes. Cut a 2 inch square from each corner of the dough. Brush the edges of the dough with beaten egg and wrap it to enclose the meat completely, lifting the ends first and then overlapping the sides.

Roll the veal onto a baking sheet so the join in the dough is underneath and brush with beaten egg glaze. Roll out the pastry dough trimmings, cut in strips and diamonds and decorate the veal with bands and leaves of dough. Brush these again with beaten egg and chill 15 minutes. Set the oven at hot (425°F).

Bake the veal in the heated oven for 30–35 minutes or until the pastry is brown and crisp and a skewer inserted in the center of the veal for 1 minute is hot to the touch when withdrawn.

To make the sauce: put the mushrooms in a buttered pan, add a squeeze of lemon juice and salt and pepper, cover and cook over high heat for 1–2 minutes or until the mushrooms are just tender. Make the velouté sauce, add the liaison of egg yolks and cream, stir in the mushrooms and taste for seasoning. Keep hot in a water bath.

When the veal is cooked, transfer it to a warm platter and serve with boiled rice. Serve the suprême sauce separately.

Spoon half the salpicon down center of crêpes, overlapping. Set veal on top, cover with remaining salpicon and crêpes

Brush edges of pastry dough with beaten egg and wrap it to enclose the veal completely

Crêpes

1 cup flour
pinch of salt
1 egg yolk
1 egg
1½ cups milk
1 tablespoon melted butter or
    oil
1 teaspoon melted butter or
    oil
1 teaspoon sugar (optional) –
    for sweet crêpes
few drops of oil

For the sweet crêpes on page 40, add 1 teaspoon sugar to the batter with the oil or butter and continue as method. Makes about 20 crêpes.

Method

Sift flour with a pinch of salt, make a well in the center and add egg yolk and whole egg. Slowly pour in milk, stirring constantly and, when half is added, stir in the melted butter or oil. Beat well until smooth. Add remaining milk, cover and let stand at room temperature for at least 30 minutes before using. The batter should be the consistency of light cream. If too thick, add a little more milk.

Heat the crêpe pan and add a few drops of oil. Add 2–3 tablespoons of batter, immediately roll it around clockwise to coat the base of the pan. (This is enough batter for a 6 inch pan.)

Cook until the bottom of the crêpe is golden, run a thin metal spatula around the edge and turn the crêpe over. Cook another 10 seconds and turn out onto a plate. Continue frying the crêpes in the same way, piling them one on top of another to keep moist.

Côtelettes d'Agneau Montrouge
(Lamb Chops Montrouge)

8 rib or loin lamb chops
2 tablespoons butter

For chicken cream
1 cup milk
3 tablespoons butter
3 tablespoons flour
1½ cups (½ lb) ground, uncooked chicken
1 egg
2 egg yolks
¼ cup heavy cream
salt and pepper

For mushroom purée
2 tablespoons butter
2 cups (½ lb) mushrooms, finely chopped
squeeze of lemon juice
1 tablespoon stock

Chop frills (see page 26)

Method
Flatten the chops slightly by pounding between 2 sheets of wax paper with a mallet or rolling pin. In a skillet melt the butter and sauté the chops gently for 1 minute on each side or until the meat is firm but not browned. Drain on paper towels.

To make the chicken cream, heat the milk with the butter, bring just to a boil, take from the heat and beat in flour all at once until the panada is smooth and thick; season. Spread on a plate to cool. Work the chicken twice through the fine blade of the grinder; then pound in a mortar and pestle until smooth and work in the panada, or work the ground chicken and panada in a blender. Beat in the egg and yolks, stir in the cream and season.

Spread the chicken cream in a mound on one side of each chop; set in a buttered baking dish, cream side up. Bake in a moderate oven (350°F) for 8–10 minutes.

To make mushroom purée: spread the butter in a pan, add the mushrooms and lemon juice and cook over high heat until all the moisture has evaporated. Season and stir in the stock.

Arrange the chops overlapping around a warm platter with bones slanting up; set a chop frill on each bone. Pile mushroom purée in center.

Côtelettes d'Agneau en Cuirasse

8 rib or loin lamb chops
1 tablespoon oil (for frying)
2 cup quantity puff pastry (see Volume 8)
1 egg, beaten to mix with ½ teaspoon salt (for glaze)

For hachis
2 tablespoons butter
1 shallot, finely chopped
2 cups (½ lb) mushrooms, finely chopped
¼ cup (2 oz) chopped cooked ham
2 teaspoons tomato paste
1 tablespoon chopped parsley

The term 'en cuirasse' (in armor) means wrapped in pastry.

Method
Make pastry dough and chill 30 minutes; set oven at hot (425°F).

Trim fat and meat from the ends of the chops to expose about 1 inch of bone, then scrape the bone ends clean. Fry the chops quickly in the oil for 1–2 minutes on each side until browned, seasoning

them after turning, or broil quickly until browned and then season. The chops should be very rare in center.

To make the hachis: melt the butter and gently fry the shallot until soft but not brown. Stir in the mushrooms and cook over high heat for 2–3 minutes until all moisture has evaporated. Take from the heat and stir in ham, tomato paste and parsley and season well. Let cool.

Roll out pastry dough to ¼ inch thickness and cut into eight 6 X 4 inch ovals. Lay a chop on each oval, top with a spoonful of hachis and brush the dough edges with beaten egg. Fold over and press the edges to seal them, leaving the end of bone sticking out. If you like, cut decorations from the pastry dough trimmings. Brush each package with egg, set on a dampened baking sheet; bake in heated oven 15–18 minutes or until the pastry is puffed and brown.

Serve with Parisienne or new potatoes and sauce chasseur.

The chops may be browned and wrapped in pastry 3–4 hours ahead and cooked just before serving, but the hachis must be chilled thoroughly before it is spooned onto the chops.

Hachis, literally meaning hash, is a finely chopped mixture of cooked meat, fish or poultry. It can have a white or brown sauce added.

Champignons Sous Cloche
(Mushrooms under Glass)

4 cups (1 lb) button mushrooms
4 thick slices of white bread (for croûtes)
½ cup butter
2 cloves of garlic, crushed
1 lemon, halved
2 tablespoons chopped parsley
salt
black pepper, freshly ground
¼ cup heavy cream

4 heatproof glass bells and dishes; 4 inch cookie cutter

Individual heatproof glass bells with matching entrée dishes or heatproof plates are used for baking in the oven. The bell not only looks attractive for serving but it also seals in the juices. The bell is not removed until the dish is served at the table so the aroma can be appreciated.

Method
Cut circles with the cookie cutter from the slices of bread. In a frying pan melt half the butter and fry the bread until golden brown on both sides; drain well on paper towels.

Trim the mushroom stems level with the caps and rub each one with a cut lemon. Squeeze the remaining lemon juice and reserve it. Cream the remaining butter and beat in lemon juice with garlic, parsley and plenty of seasoning.

Set a croûte of bread on each heatproof dish, pile the mushrooms on top and dot with the flavored butter. Spoon over the cream, cover with the bells and bake in a moderate oven (350°F) for 30 minutes or until the mushrooms are tender. Guests remove the bells at the table.

DESSERTS

Pannequets Soufflés
(Soufflé Crêpes)

1½ cup quantity of basic crêpe
  batter (see crêpe recipe,
  page 33)
2 tablespoons sugar

For vanilla soufflé filling
1¼ cups milk
1 vanilla bean or 1 teaspoon
  vanilla extract
2 tablespoons sugar
1 tablespoon flour
1 teaspoon arrowroot
2 tablespoons butter
2 egg yolks
3 egg whites
confectioners' sugar (for
  sprinkling)

In this recipe, crêpes are filled with vanilla soufflé mixture and baked in the oven so they puff up. Orange or lemon soufflé mixture (see Volume 10) will also make a delicious filling. Makes about 20 crêpes.

Method
Make the crêpe batter, adding the sugar with the eggs, and let stand 30 minutes.

To make filling: scald ¾ cup milk, add vanilla bean, if using, cover and let stand to infuse for 15 minutes. Reheat the milk until boiling, take from the heat, add sugar and vanilla extract if using, or remove the vanilla bean.

Blend reserved ½ cup milk with the flour and arrowroot to make a smooth paste. Stir into hot milk and bring to a boil, stirring constantly. Boil 2–3 seconds and take from heat. Dot top with butter, cover and let stand 5 minutes. Then stir to mix in the butter and beat in egg yolks, one at a time.

Set the oven at hot (400°F) and fry the crêpes.

Beat the egg whites until they hold a stiff peak. Heat vanilla mixture until it is warm and with a metal spoon fold in one-quarter of the whipped egg whites. Add remaining egg whites and fold them in as lightly as possible. Put a generous spoonful of mixture on 8–12 crêpes and roll them very loosely. Arrange them well spaced out in a buttered baking dish, and sprinkle generously with confectioners' sugar. Bake in heated oven 8–10 minutes or until the crêpes are puffed. Serve at once.

Watchpoint: do not wrap crêpes tightly or pack them closely in the dish because they will not have room to puff properly.

Pineapple Ninon

1 ripe pineapple

For filling
4 types of fruit from following
  selection:
2 navel oranges, rind and pith
  removed and discarded,
  sectioned
¼ lb green seedless grapes,
  stems removed
1 cup fresh cherries, pitted,
  or 1 can (8¾ oz) cherries
2 pears, pared, cored and sliced
1 pint fresh strawberries,
  hulled
2 bananas, peeled and sliced
  diagonally
2–3 tablespoons sugar (or to
  taste)
2 tablespoons kirsch

For almond pastry
½ cup flour
⅓ cup whole blanched almonds,
  ground
3 tablespoons butter, softened
3 tablespoons sugar
1 egg yolk

For serving
Chantilly cream (made with
  1 cup heavy cream, stiffly
  whipped, and flavored with
  1–1½ tablespoons sugar and
  ½ teaspoon vanilla)
spun sugar (see page 16) –
  optional

6–8 small tartlet pans; fluted
  cookie cutter, ½ inch larger
  than pans; pastry bag; large
  star tube

Method
To make almond pastry dough: sift ground almonds and flour onto a board or marble slab and make a large well in the center. Add the butter, sugar, and egg yolk and work together with the fingertips until smooth. Gradually draw in the almond mixture, working with the whole hand to form a dough, then knead until smooth. Chill 30 minutes.

Set the oven at hot (400°F).

Roll out dough and line tartlet pans, cutting out rounds with a cookie cutter. Bake blind in the heated oven for 10–12 minutes or until lightly browned. Let the pastry cool slightly, then take from the pans and transfer to a wire rack to cool completely.

To prepare pineapple: cut off and discard the top and plume, and cut out the flesh to leave a hollow shell. To do this, insert a knife at the bottom and cut a horizontal circle inside pineapple to loosen the flesh. Then with a long, serrated-edge knife held vertically, cut around the top just inside the skin of the pineapple to reach the bottom. Lift out the flesh in a cylinder and reserve pineapple shell.

Cut out core from the pineapple flesh with an apple corer and cut the flesh in chunks. Mix chunks with the 4 chosen fruits, sprinkle with sugar and kirsch, mix well, cover and let macerate at least 1 hour in the refrigerator.

To serve, set the pineapple shell on a round platter and pile the macerated fruit inside. Using a pastry bag fitted with the star tube, pipe rosettes of Chantilly cream to fill the tartlet shells, and arrange them around the pineapple.

If you like, make spun sugar and arrange a veil of it on top of the pineapple just before serving.

Pineapple Ninon is filled with macerated fruits and served with almond pastry tartlets

Marquise Alice is decorated with red currant jelly piped in a zig-zag pattern, cream rosettes and chocolate cones

Marquise Alice

5–6 large macaroons, crushed
1 tablespoon rum
1 envelope gelatin
$\frac{1}{4}$ cup water
egg custard (made with 2 cups
  milk, 3 egg yolks and
  3 tablespoons sugar)
1 egg white
$\frac{1}{4}$ cup heavy cream, whipped
  until it holds a soft shape
$\frac{1}{4}$ cup praline powder (see
  page 53)

For decoration
4 squares (4 oz) semisweet
  chocolate, chopped
1$\frac{1}{2}$ cups heavy cream, stiffly
  whipped
2 tablespoons red currant jelly

*7 inch square cake pan; paper
  decorating cone; pastry bag;
  medium star tube*

Method
Sprinkle macaroons with rum.

In a small pan sprinkle the gelatin over the water and let stand 5 minutes until spongy.

Make the custard and while still hot stir in the gelatin until dissolved and let cool, stirring occasionally. Stiffly whip the egg white.

When the custard is cool, place it over a pan of ice water and stir until it starts to set. At once fold in the lightly whipped cream with the praline powder and the stiffly whipped egg white. Pour half the mixture into the cake pan, spread with the soaked macaroons and add the remaining praline custard. Cover and chill at least 2 hours or until firmly set.

To make decorations: melt the chocolate on a plate over a pan of hot water and let stand until cool but still soft. Cut four 3 inch squares of wax paper, cut each in half diagonally to form a triangle and fold the triangles into cones as

when making a paper decorating cone; fasten the cones with adhesive tape. When the chocolate is cool but still soft, coat the inside of each paper cone evenly with chocolate, using your finger or the handle of a teaspoon. Chill until set, then carefully peel off the paper.

Turn the marquise out onto a platter and coat the top smoothly with some of the stiffly whipped cream. Melt the red currant jelly over low heat, stirring until smooth; cool, and put into a paper decorating cone. Snip off the tip and pipe the jelly in parallel straight lines about 1 inch apart across the top of the marquise.

For chocolate cones around marquise, fill soft chocolate into paper cones, smoothing the tops

To finish the marquise, draw a skewer across the piped jelly lines in alternate directions to make a zig-zag pattern

Draw a skewer or point of a paring knife across the jelly lines in alternate directions to make a zig-zag pattern.

Using a pastry bag fitted with the star tube, pipe rosettes of the remaining whipped cream in each chocolate cone and set them around the marquise, then pipe rosettes of cream around the base of the marquise.

Strawberry Marquise

1 pint fresh strawberries or
  1 package frozen
  strawberries
1 package ladyfingers
2–3 tablespoons kirsch
sugar (to taste)
1$\frac{1}{2}$ envelopes gelatin
$\frac{1}{4}$ cup water
egg custard (made with 2 cups
  milk, 3 egg yolks and 3 tablespoons sugar)
1 egg white
$\frac{3}{4}$ cup heavy cream, whipped
  until it holds a soft shape
3 tablespoons praline powder
  (see page 53)

For decoration
$\frac{3}{4}$ cup heavy cream, stiffly
  whipped
2 tablespoons red currant jelly
8–10 whole strawberries

*8 inch square cake pan; paper
  decorating cone; pastry bag;
  star tube*

Strawberry marquise is the summer version of marquise Alice, and is made with fresh strawberry purée and garnished with whole strawberries.

Method
Sprinkle the ladyfingers with the kirsch.

Purée the strawberries in a blender, first reserving some

for decoration, or work them through a food mill or sieve and add sugar to taste.

In a small pan sprinkle the gelatin over the water and let stand 5 minutes until spongy. Make the custard and while still hot stir in the gelatin until dissolved; stir in the strawberry purée and let cool, stirring occasionally. Stiffly whip the egg white.

When the custard is cool, place over a pan of ice water and stir until it starts to set. At once fold in the lightly whipped cream, praline powder and beaten egg white. Pour half the mixture into the cake pan, lay the ladyfingers on top and cover with the remaining strawberry mixture. Chill at least 2 hours or until firmly set.

To serve, turn out the marquise onto a platter and coat it with some of the stiffly whipped cream. Melt the red currant jelly over low heat, stirring until smooth; let cool and fill into a paper decorating cone. Snip off the tip and pipe the jelly in parallel straight lines about 1 inch apart across the top of the marquise. Draw a skewer or the point of a paring knife across the jelly lines in alternate directions to make a zig-zag pattern.

Using a pastry bag fitted with the star tube, pipe rosettes of remaining whipped cream around the edge and decorate with the whole strawberries.

Riz
à l'Impératrice

$\frac{1}{3}$ cup round grain rice
2$\frac{1}{2}$ cups milk
1$\frac{1}{2}$ tablespoons butter
$\frac{1}{4}$ cup sugar
1 envelope gelatin
$\frac{1}{4}$ cup water
vanilla custard (made with
    4 egg yolks, $\frac{1}{4}$ cup sugar,
    1 cup milk and $\frac{1}{2}$ teaspoon
    vanilla extract or $\frac{1}{2}$ vanilla
    bean, split)
$\frac{1}{4}$ cup chopped mixed candied
    fruit (orange, citron and
    lemon peel)
$\frac{1}{4}$ cup chopped candied
    pineapple
$\frac{1}{2}$ cup chopped candied cherries
2 tablespoons kirsch
1 cup heavy cream, whipped
    until it holds a soft shape
cold pineapple sauce
    (for serving)

*Fluted ring mold (6 cup
    capacity)*

Method
Lightly oil the mold.

In a pan simmer the rice in the milk for 35–40 minutes or until tender, stirring occasionally especially towards the end of cooking. Take from the heat and stir in the butter and sugar until dissolved. The consistency of the mixture should be thick but not solid. Let cool.

Sprinkle the gelatin over the water and let stand 5 minutes until spongy. Make the vanilla custard and stir the softened gelatin into the hot custard until dissolved. Let stand until cool, then stir into the cooled rice with the candied fruits and kirsch.

Set custard mixture over a pan of ice water and stir until the mixture starts to set. Fold in the lightly whipped cream and pour into the prepared mold. Chill at least 2 hours or until firm. To serve, unmold rice onto a platter and spoon around pineapple sauce.

For riz à l'impératrice, stir the ▶ custard mixture, candied fruits and kirsch into the cooled rice

Riz à l'impératrice is served with cold pineapple sauce poured around it
▼

Pineapple Sauce

$\frac{3}{4}$ cup finely chopped fresh
    pineapple or 1 can (8$\frac{1}{2}$ oz)
    crushed pineapple
2 tablespoons sugar (or to
    taste)
2 teaspoons cornstarch
pinch of salt
$\frac{3}{4}$ cup unsweetened pineapple
    juice
1 teaspoon lemon juice

Method
Mix the sugar with the cornstarch and salt, stir in the pineapple juice and bring to a boil, stirring. Simmer 2 minutes, take from heat, stir in the lemon juice and pineapple. Serve hot or cold.

Charlotte Malakoff

1 package ladyfingers
3 tablespoons kirsch
1 cup unsalted butter
1 cup sugar
1 cup whole blanched almonds, ground
½ cup chopped mixed candied fruit
1 cup heavy cream, whipped until it holds a soft shape
½ cup heavy cream, stiffly whipped (for decoration)

Charlotte mold or soufflé dish (5 cup capacity); pastry bag; medium star tube

The flavor of the charlotte mellows if it is made 1–2 days ahead. One pint fresh strawberries, hulled and sliced, can be substituted for the candied fruit.

Method

Line base of the mold or dish with a circle of wax paper.

Line the sides of the mold or dish with ladyfingers, trimming the edges of the fingers so they fit tightly. Sprinkle remaining ladyfingers with 1 tablespoon kirsch.

Cream the butter, gradually beat in the sugar and continue beating until the mixture is soft and light. Stir in ground almonds with the remaining kirsch and the candied fruit. **Watchpoint**: do not beat the mixture or the oil will be drawn out of the almonds.

Fold in the lightly whipped cream and spoon half the mixture into the prepared mold or dish. Cover mixture with soaked ladyfingers, add remaining almond mixture and smooth the top. Cover and chill the charlotte at least 4 hours or until firmly set.

To serve, trim the tops of the ladyfingers level with the almond mixture. Unmold the charlotte onto a platter and, using the pastry bag fitted with the star tube, cover the top with rosettes of whipped cream.

Malakoff was the decisive battle of the Crimean War, which was fought on Russian territory.

In their modern form **charlottes** were introduced by French chefs in Russia in the 19th century.

Soufflé Grand Marnier

1 large orange
8 sugar cubes
1 cup milk
3 eggs, separated
1½ tablespoons flour
1 tablespoon butter
2 egg whites
3 tablespoons sugar
3 tablespoons Grand Marnier
confectioners' sugar (for sprinkling)

Soufflé dish (1 quart capacity)

Method

Prepare soufflé dish with a collar, butter sides of dish and collar and sprinkle with sugar, discarding the excess. Set the oven at hot (425°F).

Rub the sugar cubes over the rind of orange until they are soaked with zest (oil).

Heat the milk gently with the sugar cubes until dissolved. Beat the egg yolks with flour until smooth, stir in the hot milk, pour the mixture back into pan and bring to a boil, stirring. Cook gently for 2 minutes, stirring constantly, then dot the top with butter, cover and let stand 5 minutes.

Stiffly whip the egg whites, preferably using a copper bowl, add the sugar and beat 20 seconds longer or until the mixture is glossy. Stir the Grand Marnier into orange mixture, then fold in one-quarter of the egg whites, using a metal spoon. Add the remaining egg whites and fold together as lightly as possible.

Transfer the mixture to prepared dish and bake at once in heated oven for 15–20 minutes or until the soufflé is puffed and brown. Remove the paper collar, sprinkle top with confectioners' sugar and serve at once.

To prepare the soufflé partly in advance, make the orange mixture, dot with butter and let cool. Half an hour before serving, heat the orange mixture until hot to the touch and stir in Grand Marnier. Stiffly whip the egg whites and continue as above.

Rich Chocolate Soufflé

4 squares (4 oz) semisweet chocolate, chopped
½ cup heavy cream
3 eggs, separated
½ teaspoon vanilla
2 tablespoons brandy
2 egg whites
3 tablespoons sugar
confectioners' sugar (for sprinkling)

Soufflé dish (1 quart capacity), or 4 individual soufflé dishes (each 1 cup capacity)

No flour is needed to thicken this soufflé as the chocolate is thick and rich enough.

Method

Prepare the large soufflé dish with a collar. Butter sides of the large dish and its collar or the sides of small dishes. Sprinkle with sugar, discarding excess. Set the oven at hot (425°F).

In a heavy-based pan over low heat, heat the chocolate with the cream, stirring until melted. Cook, stirring, until the mixture is thick and will just fall from the spoon.

Take from the heat and beat in egg yolks, one at a time; stir in the vanilla and brandy. Stiffly whip 5 egg whites, preferably using a copper bowl; add the sugar and beat 20 seconds longer or until glossy. Fold one-quarter into the warm chocolate mixture, using a metal spoon. Add the remaining egg whites and fold together as lightly as possible. Transfer to prepared dish or dishes and bake at once in heated oven for 8–10 minutes for small soufflés, or 15–20 minutes for the large one, or until puffed and browned. Remove the paper collar, if used, sprinkle surface with confectioners' sugar and serve at once.

To prepare partly in advance: make the chocolate mixture, cover and let cool. Half an hour before serving, heat the mixture until hot to the touch, beat the egg whites and continue as above.

Picnic menu 2 includes (from left to right): granary loaf, fresh spinach salad with mushrooms, ricotta tartlets, blender gazpacho, ham in Marsala and a bowl of fresh fruit (recipes are on pages 46—47)

PACK A PARTY PICNIC

Take your pick of the perfect picnic that is easy to prepare ahead. There is a choice of three imaginative menus with recipes including chicken salad, ham in Marsala and savory salmon tourtière.

MENU 1

Smoked Salmon Rolls with Shrimps

Chicken Salad

Rice Salad

Almond & Raspberry Flan

Crusty Top Sponge Cake

Assorted Cheeses

MENU 2

Blender Gazpacho

Ham in Marsala

Spinach Salad

Granary Loaf

Ricotta Tartlets

Fresh Fruit

MENU 3

Pâté in Aspic

Salmon Tourtière

Cucumber & Tomato Salad
(see Volume 17)

Strawberries with Orange

TIMETABLE

Day before
Cook chicken or fowl, cut meat in pieces and keep covered in refrigerator.
Make mayonnaise for salmon rolls and chicken salad. Cut lemon wedges for smoked salmon.
Cook rice and vegetables for salad and store separately in refrigerator.
Make vinaigrette dressing for rice salad.
Make and bake almond and raspberry flan and leave in ring or pan ready to carry; store in airtight container.
Make crusty top sponge cake and store in airtight container.

Morning
Mix chicken meat with mayonnaise, pack in container, decorate and chill.
Make filling and roll smoked salmon; butter wholewheat bread and pack in containers.
Mix ingredients for rice salad and pack in container.

Smoked Salmon Rolls with Shrimps

Cook, peel and coarsely chop $\frac{3}{4}$ lb shrimps. In a bowl combine $\frac{3}{4}$ cup mayonnaise with 3–4 drops of Tabasco sauce, $\frac{1}{2}$ teaspoon each of paprika and tomato paste and 1 tablespoon of heavy cream. Stir in the shrimps and spoon some of this mixture in the center of 12–14 thin slices of smoked salmon. Roll slices with 2 forks and pack in a container to carry. Serve with thin slices of buttered wholewheat bread and wedges of lemon. (This recipe was first given in Volume 9.)

Spoon shrimp mixture in center of slices of smoked salmon and roll up

Picnic drinks suggestions are on page 47.

Chicken Salad

4–5 lb roasting chicken or fowl
1 carrot, sliced
1 onion, quartered
1 stalk of celery, sliced
bouquet garni
salt
6–8 peppercorns
black pepper, freshly ground
$1\frac{1}{2}$–2 cups mayonnaise
squeeze of lemon juice (optional)
1 slice of canned pimiento, drained and cut in strips

Method
Put the chicken or fowl in a large kettle with the vegetables, bouquet garni, salt and peppercorns. Add enough cold water to reach the top of the bird's legs, cover with foil and the lid. Simmer over low heat for $1\frac{1}{4}$–$1\frac{1}{2}$ hours (about 30 minutes longer for a fowl) or until the thigh is tender and no pink juice runs out when it is pierced with a skewer. Let chicken cool in the liquid.

Drain the bird and discard the skin; take the meat from the bones. Cut the white and dark meat into pieces, keeping them separate in bowls. Season the mayonnaise well and sharpen it, if necessary, with a little lemon juice. Spoon one-quarter of the mayonnaise over each portion of chicken and toss with a fork so the meat is thoroughly coated.

To pack, arrange chicken in a container, layering the dark and white meat. If necessary, add a little water to the remaining mayonnaise to thin it and coat the chicken. Decorate the top with strips of pimiento, cover the container and chill.

Rice Salad

$1\frac{1}{4}$ cups long grain rice
1 cucumber, peeled and diced
1 large carrot, diced
1 cup diced green beans
1 cup shelled fresh peas or 1 package frozen peas, thawed
1 red bell pepper, cored, seeded and diced
2 medium tomatoes, peeled, seeded and cut in strips
$\frac{1}{2}$ cup vinaigrette dressing
salt

Method
Cook the rice in boiling salted water for 12–15 minutes, drain, rinse with hot water and spread out to dry.

Sprinkle the cucumber with salt, cover and let stand 30 minutes to draw out the juices (dégorger), then rinse and dry on paper towels.

Cook the carrot, beans and peas in boiling salted water for 6–8 minutes or until just tender, then drain, refresh and drain again. Blanch the pepper for 2 minutes in boiling salted water, drain, refresh and drain again. Add all the vegetables and tomatoes to rice and toss with vinaigrette dressing with 2 forks.

Vinaigrette Dressing

For $\frac{1}{2}$ cup: mix 2 tablespoons vinegar (any of the following types: red or white wine, cider or tarragon) with $\frac{1}{2}$ teaspoon salt and $\frac{1}{2}$ teaspoon freshly ground black pepper. Gradually add 6 tablespoons oil, preferably olive or peanut, whisking until it thickens slightly. Taste for seasoning.

Almond and raspberry flan is topped with meringue and decorated with confectioners' sugar and slivered almonds

Almond and Raspberry Flan

1 pint box fresh raspberries or
  1 package frozen raspberries,
  thawed and drained
confectioners' sugar
  (for sprinkling)
$\frac{1}{2}$ cup browned, slivered
  almonds

For almond pastry
$1\frac{1}{2}$ cups flour
6 tablespoons butter
2 tablespoons shortening
$\frac{1}{4}$ cup whole blanched almonds,
  ground
3 tablespoons sugar
1 large egg yolk or 2 small egg
  yolks
$\frac{1}{2}$ teaspoon vanilla
1–2 tablespoons cold water

For almond meringue
$\frac{1}{2}$ cup whole blanched almonds,
  ground
3 egg whites
$\frac{3}{4}$ cup sugar

*8 inch flan ring or pie pan with
  removable base*

Method

To make almond pastry: sift the flour into a bowl, add the butter and shortening and rub in with the fingertips until the mixture resembles crumbs. Stir in the ground almonds and sugar. Mix the egg yolks with the vanilla and water and add to the dry ingredients. Stir to mix, then work with the hand to a smooth dough. Chill 30 minutes. Set the oven at moderate (350°F).

Roll out the pastry dough, line the flan ring or pie pan, prick the bottom lightly and spread with the raspberries.

To make almond meringue: beat the egg whites until they hold a stiff peak. Add the sugar and beat 20–30 seconds longer or until the meringue is glossy and stands in peaks. Fold in the ground almonds.

Spread almond meringue over the raspberries and bake in heated oven for 30–35 minutes or until the pastry and meringue are browned. Transfer to a wire rack to cool.

When cold, sprinkle top of flan thickly with confectioners' sugar and scatter over the browned almonds.

To carry, leave the flan in the flan ring or pie pan and remove it to serve.

Crusty Top Sponge Cake

This recipe was first given in Volume 6.

Set oven at moderate (350°F). Grease an 8 inch springform pan, sprinkle it with sugar, then with flour and discard excess.

Sift 1 cup flour with a pinch of salt. In a bowl mix 4 egg yolks with $\frac{1}{2}$ cup sugar and 2 teaspoons orange flower water; beat with an electric beater, heavy whisk or flat wooden spoon until mixture is thick and light colored. Beat egg whites until they hold a stiff peak and beat in $\frac{1}{2}$ cup sugar, 1 tablespoon at a time, until the mixture holds a stiff peak again. With a metal spoon fold the egg white mixture alternately with the flour into the egg yolk mixture. Pour batter into the pan; bake in heated oven for 45 minutes or until the cake shrinks from the sides of the pan and the top springs back when lightly pressed with a fingertip. Turn out onto a wire rack to cool.

TIMETABLE

Day before
Prepare vegetables for gazpacho and make purée; keep in refrigerator.
Bake ham, cool and layer in container to carry, add sauce; refrigerate.
Wash spinach, dry and store in refrigerator in plastic bag. Make vinaigrette dressing.
Make and bake ricotta tartlets; store in airtight container.
Make and bake granary loaves and keep in airtight container.

Morning
Add ice water to gazpacho, pour into a vacuum flask to carry; pack garnish separately or add to soup, if you like. Add vegetables to vinaigrette dressing (but carry dressing and spinach leaves separately).
Toss salad just before serving.

Blender Gazpacho

2 green bell peppers, cored, seeded and chopped
4 medium tomatoes, peeled, seeded and chopped
2 cucumbers, peeled, seeded and diced
1 clove of garlic, crushed
$\frac{1}{2}$ onion, chopped
5 tablespoons olive oil
salt and pepper
4 cups ice water

There are many versions of this cold Spanish cucumber and tomato soup. This is a quick recipe made in the blender; for others consult the Index.

Method
Reserve $\frac{1}{4}$ cup each of the chopped peppers, tomatoes and diced cucumber for garnish. Purée the remaining pepper with the garlic and onion in a blender, add the cucumber, tomatoes and purée them also. Add the olive oil, work until emulsified, then strain the soup and season to taste with salt and pepper. Stir in the ice water with a few ice cubes and pour into a vacuum flask to carry. Pack the vegetable garnish separately or add to the flask, if you like.

Ham in Marsala

3 lb piece boneless regular ham
$\frac{1}{2}$ cup Marsala or sherry
2 tablespoons oil
2 onions, chopped
2 carrots, chopped
1 stalk of celery, chopped
1 tablespoon chopped parsley
1 cup stock
salt and pepper

Method
In a deep flameproof casserole heat the oil and sauté the onion, carrot and celery until brown. Add the parsley, stock and seasoning, put in the ham and cover with the lid. Bake in a moderate oven (350°F) for 30 minutes. Add the Marsala or sherry, baste the ham and cook 30 minutes longer. Let cool, then take the ham from the pot, carve it in thick slices and arrange it in a container to carry.

Boil the cooking liquid to reduce it to $\frac{3}{4}$ cup, season to taste and strain it, discarding any fat. Spoon this gravy over the ham, cool and seal the container.

Granary Loaf

7 cups stone-ground wholewheat flour
2 teaspoons salt
2 packages dry or 2 cakes compressed yeast
1 tablespoon sugar
$3\frac{1}{2}$–4 cups lukewarm water

2 medium loaf pans
($8\frac{1}{2}$ X $4\frac{1}{2}$ X $2\frac{1}{2}$ inches)

This wholewheat dough is mixed lightly without kneading so it only requires a few minutes to make. The quantity of water varies with the brand of flour used. Stone-ground wholewheat flour is essential.

Method
Grease loaf pans and warm them. Sift flour and salt into a large bowl and warm in a low oven so yeast will work more quickly.

Put $\frac{1}{2}$ cup of the lukewarm water with the sugar and yeast in a bowl and let stand 5 minutes until dissolved. Make a well in the center of the flour, add the yeast mixture with the remaining warm water and stir with a wooden spoon until the flour is evenly moistened. The dough should be so wet that it is slippery.

Spoon the dough into the warmed pans, cover with a damp cloth and leave in a warm place for 1 hour or until doubled in bulk.

Set the oven at moderately hot (375°F).

Bake the loaves in heated oven for 50 minutes or until they sound hollow when tapped. Cool on a wire rack.

Ricotta Tartlets

For pastry
$1\frac{1}{2}$ cups flour
pinch of salt
3 tablespoons butter
3 tablespoons shortening
3–4 tablespoons water

For filling
$1\frac{1}{2}$ cups ($\frac{3}{4}$ lb) ricotta cheese or creamed cottage cheese
3 eggs
$\frac{1}{2}$ cup sugar
1 teaspoon vanilla
$\frac{1}{4}$ cup mixed chopped candied fruits

12–16 tartlet pans

Method
Make pastry dough as for pie pastry and chill 30 minutes. Set oven at hot (400°F).

To make the filling: work the cheese through a sieve and beat it until soft. Beat in the eggs and sugar, then stir in vanilla and candied fruits.

Roll out dough and line the tartlet pans. Fill with the cheese mixture. Bake in heated oven for 15–20 minutes or until brown.

Spinach Salad

¾ lb fresh spinach, washed,
 dried, and stems removed
3 scallions, finely sliced
1 cup (¼ lb) mushrooms,
 finely sliced
½ cup vinaigrette dressing
 made with lemon juice
 instead of vinegar
 (see page 44)

Method
Add the scallions and mushrooms to the vinaigrette dressing. Carry dressing and spinach
in separate containers and
toss them together just before
serving.

Picnic Drinks

Drinks are important at any
picnic and the hotter the day
the more vital they become.
Take plenty of cola, soda and
a vacuum flask of fresh iced
lemonade for children and
something stronger for the
adults like a chilled white
wine cup.

Moselle Wine Cup

Chill 1 bottle of white wine
(Moselle) and combine with
½ cup dry sherry and the
grated rinds of ½ orange
and ½ lemon. Add sliced or
diced fruits with about 3 tablespoons confectioners' sugar, if
you like. Stir to dissolve the
sugar and chill. Carry in a
vacuum flask and serve over
ice cubes. Fill each glass with
chilled club soda just before
serving — you will need about
1½ quarts.

MENU 3

Pâté in Aspic

Salmon Tourtière

*Cucumber &
Tomato Salad
(see Volume 17)*

*Strawberries
with Orange*

TIMETABLE

Day before
Make pâté and chill; coat with aspic and store in refrigerator, tightly covered.
Make salmon tourtière, cool in pan, wrap tightly and store, covered, in pan in refrigerator.
Make vinaigrette dressing for cucumber and tomato salad.

Morning
Make cucumber and tomato salad, chill, and pack in insulated container.
Make strawberries with orange, chill thoroughly and pack them in an insulated container.

Picnic drinks suggestions are on page 47.

Pâté in Aspic

$\frac{1}{2}$ lb calves liver
$\frac{1}{2}$ lb chicken or pigs liver
béchamel sauce, made with
    3 tablespoons butter,
    3 tablespoons flour, 1$\frac{1}{2}$ cups
    milk (infused with slice of
    onion, 6 peppercorns,
    blade of mace and bay leaf)
$\frac{1}{2}$ teaspoon mixed dried herbs
    (thyme, rosemary, sage)
pinch of ground mace
1 thick slice ($\frac{1}{4}$ lb) of ham,
    or Canadian bacon, diced
salt and pepper
tarragon leaves or sprigs of
    parsley, blanched
    (for decoration)

For aspic
$\frac{1}{2}$ envelope gelatin
1 can consommé
1$\frac{1}{2}$ tablespoons sherry

*6–8 individual heatproof dishes
or custard cups*

Carry and serve pâté in the dishes or cups.

Method
Make the béchamel sauce, season well and spread on a plate to cool.

Remove skin and ducts from liver, cut in pieces, work through the fine blade of a grinder and combine with béchamel sauce; alternatively, purée liver and sauce in a blender; work through a sieve to remove liver ducts.

Add herbs, mace and ham or Canadian bacon to mixture, season well and spoon into the dishes or cups until they are three-quarters full. Tap firmly to dispel any air bubbles. Cover each dish or cup with buttered foil and set in a water bath in a small roasting pan. Bake in a moderate oven (350°F) for 40–50 minutes or until firm to the touch. Chill overnight.

To make aspic: sprinkle gelatin over $\frac{1}{4}$ cup of the consommé in a small pan. Let stand 5 minutes or until spongy, then dissolve over a pan of hot water and stir into remaining consommé with sherry. Fill each mold with a layer of aspic, reserving half, and chill until set. Decorate each mold with a leaf of tarragon or parsley, add another layer of aspic to each mold and chill again.

Salmon Tourtière

2 lb salmon steaks or fillets
$\frac{1}{2}$ cup long grain rice, boiled,
    drained and dried (see rice
    salad on page 44)
4 hard-cooked eggs, chopped
1 tablespoon chopped mixed
    herbs (parsley, tarragon,
    chives, dill)
salt and pepper
1 egg, beaten to mix
pinch of ground mace
1 egg, beaten to mix (for glaze)

For rich pie pastry
3 cups flour
$\frac{1}{2}$ teaspoon salt
$\frac{1}{2}$ cup butter
$\frac{1}{2}$ cup shortening
2 egg yolks
5–6 tablespoons water

8 inch springform pan

Method
Prepare pastry dough and chill 30 minutes.

Remove skin and bones from uncooked salmon, keeping flesh in as large pieces as possible. Chop any trimmings and mix with rice, hard-cooked eggs, herbs, seasoning and beaten egg.

Set oven at hot (400°F). Roll out just over half the dough and line the pan. Put a layer of rice mixture in bottom of pan and lay salmon pieces on top. Season with salt, pepper and mace and cover with remaining rice.

Roll out remaining dough, cover pie, seal and trim the edges. Brush with beaten egg and decorate with pastry trimmings.

Bake in heated oven for 25 minutes or until pastry is lightly browned. Lower oven heat to moderate (350°F) and bake 15–20 minutes longer or until a skewer inserted in the center for 1 minute is hot to the touch when withdrawn. Take from the oven and cool in the pan. Leave in the pan and pack in airtight container to carry. Cut in wedges to serve.

Strawberries with Orange

This recipe was first given in Volume 3; this version serves 6 people.

Hull 2 quarts strawberries and place in a bowl. Rub 12–16 sugar cubes over the rind of 3 oranges until they are soaked with the oil, then crush the cubes. Squeeze juice from oranges and combine with crushed sugar and $\frac{1}{2}$ cup of brandy. Stir until the sugar is dissolved and pour over the strawberries. Cover and chill thoroughly for 2–3 hours before serving.

Salmon tourtière, rich pie pastry with a salmon, rice and egg filling, is served in wedges

Gâteau Mercédès is decorated with slivered almonds (recipe is on page 54)

EUROPEAN GATEAUX AND PASTRIES

France and Austria are renowned for their cakes and pastries but several other European countries have specialties that can compete on equal terms. Sachertorte from Vienna, for instance – chocolate cake with a special frosting – is world famous; Prinsesstarta from Denmark, with marzipan flowers, is a pretty cake shaped like a child's flowered straw hat without a brim. And Doboz torte is a delicious chocolate and caramel cake from Hungary.

These cakes are not easy to make but the results illustrate one of the most highly-prized skills of the professional chef. The art lies in measuring ingredients exactly so basic mixtures are perfectly balanced, then assembling them as meticulously as possible so the cakes look as good as they taste. For more French gâteaux and pastries, see Volume 14.

Basic Recipes

These basic recipes, fillings and decorations were given in the first feature on French gâteaux and pastries in Volume 14 and are repeated here for your convenience. For more detailed notes, please refer back to Volume 14.

Basic Génoise

For 3 egg quantity
3 eggs
¼ cup butter
½ cup sugar
½ cup cake flour
pinch of salt
½ teaspoon vanilla

8–9 inch moule à manqué or 7–8 inch springform pan

For more general advice read the feature on sponge cakes in Volume 6. Génoise is a type of sponge cake with butter added for richness.

Method
Set oven at moderate (350°F). Grease the mold or pan, line the bottom with a circle of wax paper, grease it again, sprinkle with sugar, then with flour and discard the excess.

Sift flour and salt 2–3 times. Warm butter in a bowl or pan over hot water until it is very soft and pourable. **Watchpoint:** take great care that the butter does not become hot or oily.

Break eggs into a large bowl (preferably copper) and gradually beat in sugar with a balloon whisk, electric beater or rotary beater. Set bowl over a pan of boiling water but not touching the water; take pan from the heat. Beat sugar and eggs for 10–12 minutes or until the mixture is

light and thick enough to leave a ribbon trail on itself when the beater is lifted. Take bowl off the pan, add vanilla and continue whisking 5 minutes or until the mixture is cold. If using an electric beater, no heat is necessary.

Sift one-third of the flour over the batter and fold it in with a metal spoon. Next fold in half the remaining flour, then the butter, quickly followed by the remaining flour.

Transfer batter to the prepared pan and bake in heated oven for 25–30 minutes or until the cake shrinks slightly from the sides of pan and the top springs back when lightly pressed with a fingertip. Turn out onto a wire rack to cool.

Basic French Flan Pastry

For 1 cup quantity
scant 1 cup flour
¼ cup butter
¼ cup sugar
2 egg yolks
½ teaspoon vanilla

Makes enough to line a 7–8 inch flan ring, or 9–12 individual tartlet pans (depending on size). Vanilla sugar can be used instead of plain sugar and vanilla extract in this recipe (see box on page 66).

Method
Sift the flour onto a board or marble slab and make a large well in the center. Add the butter, sugar, egg yolks and vanilla, if used, and work together with the fingertips until smooth. Gradually draw in the flour, working with the whole hand to form a dough, then knead until smooth. Chill 1–2 hours before using.

Quantity Terms

Terms like 1 cup quantity pastry or 1 cup quantity butter cream frosting refer to the amount obtained by using 1 cup of the principal ingredient at the top of the ingredient list, not 1 cup of prepared pastry dough or butter cream frosting.

FILLINGS AND DECORATIONS

Fondant Icing

For 2 cup quantity
2 cups sugar
¾ cup water
2 tablespoons corn syrup, or pinch of cream of tartar (dissolved in 1 teaspoon water)

Sugar thermometer

Fondant keeps well for 3–4 weeks in an airtight container.

Method
To make fondant: place sugar and water in a large saucepan over low heat and dissolve sugar slowly, following the rules for sugar boiling in the feature on candies in Volume 13. When dissolved add corn syrup or dissolved cream of tartar, bring to a boil and boil steadily to the soft ball stage (240°F–242°F on a sugar thermometer). Take pan at once from heat, let bubbles subside and pour mixture slowly onto a dampened marble slab or into a dampened roasting pan.

Cool mixture slightly, add chosen flavoring and then pull batch together with a sugar scraper or metal spatula, taking the mixture from edge to center. Leave until fondant feels just warm to the touch. If using a roasting pan, turn out onto a Formica-type surface. Work vigorously with a sugar scraper or metal spatula in one hand and a wooden spoon in the other, turning and pulling it to the center until it becomes creamy – it will do this suddenly and become too stiff to work.

Then take a small piece of fondant at a time and work it with the fingers until smooth. Pack firm fondant in balls into a bowl or jar, cover tightly and let stand at least 1 hour and preferably 2–3 days to mellow before use.

To use Fondant for Icing

The consistency of finished fondant will vary from soft and pliable to stiff and almost hard, depending on the exact temperature to which it was boiled and the humidity of the atmosphere. Put the fondant in the top of a double boiler or in a bowl in a pan of hot water. Add a few spoonsful sugar syrup (made by dissolving 1 cup sugar in ½ cup water, bringing to a boil and boiling for 2 minutes). Heat the mixture until it is lukewarm, stirring until smooth and adding more sugar syrup as necessary so the warm fondant coats the back of a spoon. Add a few drops of food coloring, if you like. **Watchpoint:** do not let fondant get too hot or it will lose its gloss. Add food coloring sparingly if you want a pastel shade.

Set the cake to be coated on a wire rack over a tray or plate to catch the drips. Brush the cake with apricot jam glaze and let stand a few minutes to set. Pour the warm fondant all at once on top of the cake and spread it quickly with a metal spatula, working down the sides. Do not continue working the fondant on top of the cake after it starts to set or the finish will be rough. If necessary, the sides can be patched, then smoothed with a metal spatula dipped in hot water.

Glacé Icing

For 2 cups: sift $2\frac{1}{2}$ cups confectioners' sugar into a bowl. Add 2–4 tablespoons water, stirring to make a smooth, fairly stiff paste. Heat icing over a pan of hot water until lukewarm – it should coat the back of a wooden spoon. If not, add a little more water or beat in more sifted confectioners' sugar. If you like, flavor with a little vanilla or few drops of lemon juice.

Royal Icing

For 1 cup: sift $1\frac{3}{4}$ cups ($\frac{1}{2}$ lb) confectioners' sugar. Beat 1 egg white until frothy and beat in the confectioners' sugar, 1 tablespoon at a time. Continue beating until the mixture will stand in peaks. Beat in 1 teaspoon lemon juice.

Butter Cream Frosting 1

For $\frac{3}{4}$ cup quantity
$\frac{3}{4}$ cup unsalted butter
2 egg yolks
$\frac{1}{4}$ cup sugar
$\frac{1}{4}$ cup water

To flavor (optional)
1 teaspoon vanilla
grated rind of $\frac{1}{2}$ orange or 1 lemon
2 teaspoons dry instant coffee (or to taste)
2–3 squares (2–3 oz) semisweet chocolate, melted over hot water and left until cool but still liquid

Method
In a bowl beat the egg yolks lightly until mixed. Dissolve the sugar in the water, bring to a boil and boil until the syrup spins a thread when a little is lifted on a spoon (230°F–234°F on a sugar thermometer). Gradually pour the hot syrup onto the egg yolks, beating constantly, and continue beating until the mixture is cool and thick and light. Cream the butter and gradually beat in the egg and sugar mixture. Flavor to taste with vanilla, orange or lemon rind, coffee or chocolate. **Note**: if you like, flavor the butter cream with vanilla and use what you need. Flavor the rest with coffee and use it; then flavor the remaining butter cream with chocolate. This last portion will blend all 3 flavors but the predominant flavor will be chocolate.

Note: do not reduce quantities to make smaller gâteaux because it is impossible to measure smaller quantities accurately.

Butter Cream Frosting 2

For 1 cup quantity
1 cup unsalted butter
2 egg whites
1 cup confectioners' sugar

Method
Sift the confectioners' sugar onto a sheet of wax paper. Have ready a pan of simmering water. Beat the egg whites with a rotary or electric beater until frothy. Beat in the sifted sugar a teaspoon at a time. If beating by hand, set the bowl over hot water and continue beating until the mixture forms a tall peak when the beater is lifted; take from the heat and continue beating until cool. If using an electric beater, no heat is needed.

Cream the butter and beat the meringue mixture into it, a little at a time. Flavor and color as required.

Apricot Jam Glaze

Method
In a saucepan bring slowly to a boil 12 oz of apricot jam with the juice of $\frac{1}{2}$ lemon and 2 tablespoons water. Stir until smooth, simmer 5 minutes, strain and return to the pan. Boil 5 minutes more and pour into a jar for storage. If for immediate use, continue boiling until thick. If using a smooth jam or jelly with no pieces of fruit, do not add water.

Meringue Italienne

It is impossible to make less than a 2 egg white quantity of meringue, so when a 1 egg white quantity is called for, use the rest of the meringue for another purpose.

For 2 egg white quantity: in a saucepan heat $\frac{1}{2}$ cup sugar with $\frac{1}{2}$ cup water until the sugar is dissolved, bring to a boil and boil until the syrup forms a thread when tested between finger and thumb (234°F on a sugar thermometer). Stiffly beat 2 egg whites and gradually pour in the hot syrup, beating constantly. Continue beating until the meringue is cool and stiff enough to hold a shape.

Praline Powder

For about $\frac{1}{2}$ cup: put $\frac{1}{2}$ cup unblanched almonds and $\frac{1}{2}$ cup sugar in a heavy-based pan. Cook over low heat until the sugar melts, shaking pan occasionally. When the sugar turns a pale golden brown, stir the mixture with a metal spoon and continue cooking until it is dark brown, but do not let it burn. Pour at once onto an oiled baking sheet; leave until cold and hard.

Grind in a rotary cheese grater or a grinder or work in a blender a little at a time. Praline powder can be stored in an airtight container – it may become soft and sticky, but flavor will not be impaired.

FRENCH

Gâteau Mercédès

2 cup quantity French flan pastry

For almond filling
2 cups whole blanched
   almonds, ground
1 cup sugar
4 egg whites
1 tablespoon kirsch
$\frac{1}{2}$ cup mixed candied fruits,
   finely chopped
$\frac{1}{4}$ cup apricot jam
$\frac{1}{2}$ cup slivered almonds
$\frac{1}{3}$ cup apricot jam glaze

8 inch springform pan

Method
Make pastry dough and chill 30 minutes. Set oven at moderate (350°F).

To make almond filling: in a bowl pound the ground almonds and sugar with the end of a rolling pin and gradually work in the egg whites; when very smooth beat in the kirsch. Alternatively, work the almonds and sugar with the egg whites in a blender until smooth and add the kirsch.

Mix the candied fruits with the jam.

Roll out the dough, line the springform pan and prick the bottom with a fork. Spread the candied fruit mixture in the bottom and fill the pan with the almond mixture. Sprinkle the slivered almonds on top.

Bake in heated oven for 45 minutes or until the gâteau is brown and a skewer inserted in the center comes out clean.

Let cool in the pan, then unmold the gâteau and brush the top generously with melted apricot jam glaze.

For the gâteau Mercédès first line springform pan with the French flan pastry dough

Put candied fruits in the pastry shell and pour the almond filling on top

Gâteau Pithiviers
(Pithiviers cake)

2 cup quantity puff pastry
   (see Volume 8)
1 egg, beaten with $\frac{1}{2}$ teaspoon
   salt (for glaze)

For almond filling
1 cup whole blanched
   almonds, ground
3 tablespoons butter
$\frac{1}{2}$ cup sugar
2 egg yolks
$\frac{1}{2}$ teaspoon vanilla or
   1 tablespoon orange flower
   water or rum

This gâteau is a specialty of the town of Pithiviers in the Loire valley of France. For the filling to have the best texture, the almonds must be pounded thoroughly to bring out the oil before the other ingredients are added.

Method
Make the puff pastry and chill thoroughly.

To make the almond filling: pound the ground almonds in a mortar and pestle until they are smooth and paste-like. In a bowl cream the butter, gradually beat in the sugar and continue beating until the mixture is soft and light. Beat in the ground almonds, then the egg yolks and flavoring and continue beating until the mixture is light colored. Set the oven at hot (400°F).

Divide the pastry into one-third and two-thirds, and roll each portion into 6–7 inch rounds; the larger portion will be twice as thick as the smaller one. Place the thinner round of pastry on a lightly dampened baking sheet and spread it with the almond mixture, leaving an inch border of pastry around. Brush the border with water, place the thicker round of pastry on top and press the edges firmly together. Mark the edges with the back of a knife to seal and indent them. Brush the top with beaten egg, making sure none drips down the sides of the pastry and prevents it from rising. Mark the top of the gâteau with the back of a knife in decreasing circles, then, using the back of the knife again, draw lines from the center of the gâteau to the edge to give six sections. Make a hole in the center to let steam escape and chill 30 minutes.

Bake the gâteau in the heated oven for 20–30 minutes or until it is puffed and brown.

Note: for gâteau and pastry basic recipes, fillings and decorations, see pages 52–53.

Quantity Terms

Terms like 1 cup quantity pastry or 1 cup quantity butter cream frosting refer to the amount obtained by using 1 cup of the principal ingredient at the top of the ingredient list, not 1 cup of prepared pastry dough or butter cream frosting.

Gâteau Pithiviers is a specialty of the town Pithiviers in the Loire valley, France

Gâteau Mousseline à l'Orange
(Orange Mousseline Cake)

½ cup sugar
finely grated rind of 2 oranges
4 egg yolks
few drops of red food coloring
6 tablespoons flour
6 tablespoons arrowroot
3 egg whites

To finish
⅓ cup apricot jam glaze
2 cup quantity fondant icing
    flavored with 2 tablespoons
    orange juice
candied orange peel cut in
    crescents or diamonds

*8–9 inch moule à manqué or
springform pan*

Method
Grease and flour the pan and set the oven at moderate (350°F). Sift the flour and arrowroot together several times. Work the sugar with the orange rind until well mixed, beat in the egg yolks one by one and continue beating until the mixture is thick and light. Color it light pink with a few drops of red food coloring.

Stiffly beat the egg whites. Fold the flour mixture and egg whites alternately into the orange mixture in 2–3 batches as lightly as possible. Pour into the prepared pan and bake in the heated oven for 25–30 minutes or until the cake springs back when lightly pressed with a fingertip.

Turn out cake on a wire rack to cool, then brush with melted apricot jam glaze and, when set, coat with orange fondant icing. Decorate the top of the cake with crescents or diamonds of candied orange peel.

A **moule à manqué** is a French cake pan with deep, sloping—as opposed to straight—sides.

It is said to have been named by a Paris pâtissier who criticized a cake mixture made by his chief baker. The baker, who didn't like his cake called a failure (un manqué), added butter, covered the cake with praline and sold it to a customer, who came back for more. It was then christened 'un manqué' and a special mold was designed for it.

These pans are good for cakes to be iced because icing runs easily down the sloping sides.

Quantity Terms

Terms like 1 cup quantity pastry or 1 cup quantity butter cream frosting refer to the amount obtained by using 1 cup of the principal ingredient at the top of the ingredient list, not 1 cup of prepared pastry dough or butter cream frosting.

Gâteau Alcazar

1 cup quantity French flan
    pastry
⅓ cup apricot jam glaze

For 1 cup quantity almond
    mousse filling
1 cup whole blanched almonds,
    ground
½ cup sugar
3 eggs
½ teaspoon vanilla
2 tablespoons kirsch
¼ cup melted butter

For almond decoration
1 cup whole blanched almonds,
    ground
½ cup sugar
1 egg white, beaten until frothy
¼ cup apricot jam glaze
6–8 shelled pistachios,
    blanched and halved

*8 inch moule à manqué or
springform pan; pastry bag;
¼ inch plain tube*

The decoration of this gâteau is reminiscent of the grilles in the famous Spanish palace, the Alcazar.

Method
Make pastry dough and chill 30 minutes, then roll out and line the moule à manqué or springform pan, trimming dough level with moule à manqué but three-eighths inch below sides of springform pan. Prick the bottom of the dough and spread with one-third cup apricot jam glaze. Set the oven at moderately hot (375°F).

To make the almond mousse filling: in a mortar and pestle or in a bowl, using the end of a rolling pin, pound the ground almonds with the sugar until slightly paste-like. Add 1 egg, vanilla and kirsch and beat until thick and light colored. Alternatively, work the almonds, sugar, 1 egg, vanilla and kirsch in a blender.

Separate the remaining eggs and beat the yolks, one by one, into the mixture until it is thick. Stiffly whip egg whites. Fold melted butter into almond mixture, then fold in the egg whites.

Watchpoint: fold the mixture as lightly as possible, using a metal spoon to cut the mixture cleanly without knocking out air bubbles.

Pour almond mousse into the lined moule à manqué or springform pan and bake in heated oven for 35–40 minutes or until browned and a skewer inserted in the center comes out clean. Unmold it and leave to cool on a wire rack.

Turn down the oven to moderate (350°F).

To make almond decoration: pound the almonds with the sugar until paste-like, then beat in enough egg white to make a smooth paste that still holds its shape. Alternatively, work the almonds and sugar with the egg white in a blender.

Put the almond mixture into a pastry bag fitted with the plain tube and pipe the mixture on top of the cake in a diamond-shaped lattice. Bake the cake in heated oven for 10 minutes longer or until the almond decoration is lightly browned.

Watchpoint: be careful not to burn the cake.

Put ¼ cup apricot jam glaze in a pan and reduce until very thick. Brush it in each diamond of the lattice. Place half a pistachio in each diamond.

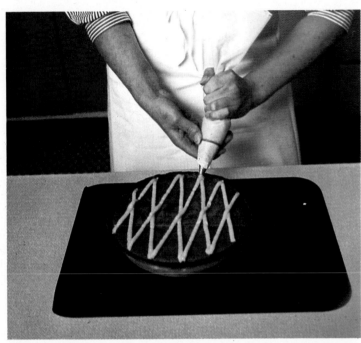

◀ *To finish gâteau Alcazar, pipe the almond mixture on top of the cake in a diamond-shaped lattice*

Gâteau Alcazar — made with French flan pastry and an almond mousse filling — is decorated with a lattice pattern and halved pistachios

Gâteau Mexicaine

¾ cup flour
pinch of salt
¼ cup butter
5 tablespoons cocoa
1 cup water
4 eggs
½ cup sugar
½ cup quantity chocolate butter
  cream frosting 1 or 2
½ cup apricot jam glaze
2 cup quantity fondant or 2 cups
  glacé icing, flavored with
  1½ squares (1½ oz) melted
  semisweet chocolate
1 cup white royal icing

*9 inch springform pan; paper
decorating cone*

Method

Set oven at moderate (350°F)
and grease pan.

Sift flour with salt. Warm
butter in a bowl over hot water
until it is soft enough to pour
easily but is not oily. Mix
cocoa with water in a small
pan and cook over low heat,
stirring, until it is thick and
creamy. Let cool.

Beat the eggs until mixed
and gradually add sugar, beating constantly. Set the bowl
over a pan of hot water and
continue beating until the
mixture is thick and light and
leaves a ribbon trail when the
beater is lifted. Take from heat
and continue beating until
mixture is cool. If using an
electric beater, no heat is
necessary.

Stir in the cocoa mixture,
then fold in two-thirds of the
sifted flour. Finally fold in the
remaining flour with the butter.
Watchpoint: the folding of
flour and butter must be done
lightly and quickly, using a
metal spoon to cut the mixture cleanly without knocking out air bubbles.

Pour cake batter into the
prepared pan and bake in

heated oven for 40–45 minutes or until it springs back
when lightly pressed with a
fingertip. Cool on a wire rack.
Cut in two and sandwich with
chocolate butter cream frosting. Brush all over with apricot
jam glaze and leave until set.

Put the royal icing into a
paper decorating cone and cut
off the tip. Pour the fondant or
glacé icing over the cake to
coat it completely and, before
the icing is set, pipe parallel
lines of royal icing about 1
inch apart across the top.
Quickly draw the point of a
knife across the cake at right
angles to the lines, working
first one way, then the other,
to give a zig-zag effect.

Gâteau Progrès
(Progress Cake)

For white japonais
5 egg whites
1 cup sugar
1⅓ cups whole blanched
  almonds, ground
¾ cup quantity butter
  cream frosting 1
4 squares (4 oz) semisweet
  chocolate, chopped and
  melted
½ cup quantity praline powder
  (see page 53)

To finish
½ cup slivered almonds,
  browned and finely
  chopped
confectioners' sugar (for
  sprinkling)

*Pastry bag and ¼ inch plain
tube*

Method

Mark 8-inch circles on 5
sheets of silicone paper and
set them on baking sheets.
Set the oven at moderate
(350°F). Make the japonais
meringue mixture (see box).

Spoon one-fifth of the
japonais mixture onto each
sheet of paper and spread in
8-inch circles. Bake in the
heated oven, one or two
rounds at a time, for about
10 minutes or until very
lightly browned. Trim the
rounds neatly with a knife
while still hot, then let cool
to tepid, peel off the paper and
transfer them to a wire rack.

Make the butter cream
frosting and add the melted,
cooled chocolate. Beat the
praline powder into the chocolate butter cream frosting,
reserving 2 tablespoons frosting for decoration.

When all the almond
rounds are cold, sandwich
them with the praline butter

cream frosting and spread the
rest on the top and sides of the
cake. Sprinkle the top thickly
with confectioners' sugar.
Press the chopped browned
almonds around the sides. Fill
the reserved chocolate butter
cream frosting into a pastry
bag, fitted with a ¼ inch plain
tube, and pipe 'PROGRÈS'
across the top of the cake.

Japonais Meringue Mixture

For this meringue mixture,
ground almonds are
folded with the sugar into
the egg whites. The
almonds may be just
blanched and ground for
a white japonais, or they
may be toasted until
brown before grinding.

To make japonais merin-
gue mixture: work ground
almonds and sugar
together through a coarse
sieve, using quantities
specified in the individual
recipe. Stiffly whip egg
whites and fold in the
almond mixture. On a
baking sheet lined with
silicone paper, shape and
bake the japonais accord-
ing to the individual recipe.
Let cool until tepid, then
peel off paper and transfer
to a wire rack to cool
completely.

Gâteau Nougatine
(Nougat Cake)

about ¾ cup crushed nougat
(see right)
½ cup shelled hazelnuts,
browned and ground
1 cup cake flour
pinch of salt
¼ cup butter
4 eggs
½ cup sugar
¾ cup quantity butter
cream frosting 1
1 cup quantity fondant icing
flavored with 1 square (1 oz)
semisweet chocolate
chopped and melted
crescents of nougat (for
decoration)

*9–10 inch moule à manqué or
9 inch springform pan*

Method
Grease moule à manqué or
pan, line the bottom with a
circle of wax paper, grease it
again, sprinkle with flour and
discard the excess. Set oven
at moderate (350°F).

Sift the flour 2–3 times with
the salt. Warm the butter in a
bowl or pan over a pan of hot
water until it is very soft and
pourable, taking care it does
not become hot or oily.

Break the eggs into a large
bowl, gradually beat in the
sugar, set the bowl over a
pan of hot water and beat until
the mixture is light and thick
enough to leave a ribbon trail
on itself when the beater is
lifted. Take the bowl from
the heat and continue beating
5 minutes or until the mixture
is cool. If using an electric
beater, no heat is necessary.

Fold the flour into the mixture, one-third at a time, then
fold in the warmed butter with
the ground hazelnuts. Pour
the mixture into the prepared
pan and bake in the heated

oven for 40–45 minutes or
until the top springs back
when lightly pressed with a
fingertip. Turn the cake out on
a wire rack to cool.

Beat half the crushed
nougat into the butter cream
frosting. Split the cake in 3
layers and sandwich them
with thin layers of butter
cream and nougat mixture.
Coat the top of the cake with
chocolate fondant icing and
spread the remaining frosting
around the sides. Press the
remaining crushed nougat
into the frosted sides of the
cake and decorate the cake
with crescents of nougat.

Quantity Terms

Terms like 1 cup quantity
pastry or 1 cup quantity
butter cream frosting refer
to the amount obtained by
using 1 cup of the prin-
cipal ingredient at the top
of the ingredient list, not
1 cup of prepared pastry
dough or butter cream
frosting.

Nougat

1 cup slivered almonds, finely
chopped
¾ cup sugar
1 lemon, brushed with oil

1½–2½ inch round cookie cutter

Method
Toast the almonds in a moderately hot oven (375°F) for
4–5 minutes or until lightly
browned. Oil a marble slab or
baking sheet.

Heat the sugar in a heavy-
based pan or skillet until
melted, then cook, stirring
occasionally, to a golden
brown caramel. Gradually stir
in the almonds with a metal
spoon, pour the nougat onto
the oiled marble or baking
sheet and roll it to ¼–⅛ inch
thickness with the oiled
lemon. While nougat is still
warm, cut it into crescents
with a small round cookie
cutter, then let cool until firm.
Watchpoint: work quickly
once the nougat is cooked. If
it cools and hardens too
quickly, warm it in the oven
for a few minutes.

Reserve the crescents for
decoration and crush the
remaining nougat in a mortar
and pestle or pass through the
coarse blade of a grinder.

Gâteau Pistache
(Pistachio Cake)

¼ cup shelled pistachios,
blanched
3 egg quantity Génoise cake
batter
¾ cup quantity butter cream
frosting 1
¼ cup shelled pistachios,
blanched
½ cup apricot jam glaze
1½ cups glacé icing
1 tablespoon kirsch (for
flavoring)
few whole shelled pistachios
(for decoration)

*8–9 inch moule à manqué or
8 inch springform pan*

Method
Make and bake the Génoise
and turn it out on a wire rack
to cool.

Pound the blanched pista-
chios to a paste in a mortar
and pestle and beat the paste
into the butter cream frosting.
Split the cake in two and
sandwich with the frosting.
Brush the cake with melted
apricot jam glaze, let set,
then coat with glacé icing
flavored with the kirsch.
Decorate the top with the
whole pistachios.

Gâteau Réligieuse is so called because it resembles the skirts of a nun's habit

Gâteau Réligieuse
(Nun's Cake)

French flan pastry made with $\frac{1}{2}$ cup flour, 2 tablespoons butter, 2 tablespoons sugar, 1 egg yolk, $\frac{1}{4}$ teaspoon vanilla
choux pastry made with $\frac{1}{2}$ cup flour, pinch of salt, $\frac{1}{2}$ cup water, $\frac{1}{4}$ cup butter and $1\frac{1}{2}$–2 eggs
2 cup quantity fondant icing flavored with 2–3 teaspoons dry instant coffee
1 square (1 oz) semisweet chocolate, chopped
Chantilly cream made with 2 cups heavy cream, stiffly whipped and flavored with $1\frac{1}{2}$–2 tablespoons sugar and 1 teaspoon vanilla

For sugar syrup
1 cup sugar
$\frac{1}{2}$ cup of water
small pinch of cream of tartar

Pastry bag; $\frac{1}{2}$ inch and small plain tubes; medium star tube

Method
Chill French flan pastry dough for 30 minutes. Set oven at moderately hot (375°F).

Roll out flan pastry dough to an 8-inch circle, transfer it to a baking sheet and bake in the heated oven for 15–20 minutes until pale golden. While still hot, trim the edges with a sharp knife, using a pan lid as guide, and transfer to a rack to cool.

Leave oven set at 375°F.

Make the choux pastry and put in a pastry bag fitted with a $\frac{1}{2}$ inch plain tube. On a dampened baking sheet, pipe 8–10 4-inch lengths to make éclairs, making sure they are all equal. Pipe one 3-inch circle of dough and one puff 2 inches high. Bake 10 min-

utes in the heated oven, then raise the temperature to 425°F and continue baking for about 15 minutes. When choux pastry is really firm and crisp, prick the sides to release steam and cool on a wire rack. Slit the éclairs at the sides and make small holes in the circle and puff.

Put two-thirds of the Chantilly cream into a pastry bag fitted with a small plain tube and fill the éclairs, circle and puff with cream.

Melt the coffee fondant icing and dip half the éclairs and the puff into the icing to coat one side. Melt the chocolate on a heatproof plate over a pan of hot water and stir it into the icing. Coat the remaining éclairs and the circle with chocolate fondant.

For the syrup: heat the sugar with the water until dissolved add cream of tartar and boil rapidly until the syrup is a pale golden caramel (310°F–312°F on a sugar thermometer). Stop boiling by dipping bottom of the pan in cold water, then tilt pan by lifting one side onto a cloth.

Dip one end of an éclair in syrup and set it upright on the French flan pastry round (see photograph). Dip the end and one side of an éclair with different icing in syrup and set it beside the first so the syrup sticks them together. Continue, using all the éclairs to make a circle, alternating the kinds of icing and ensure the éclairs lean slightly inwards at the top. Dip the choux pastry circle in syrup and set it on top of the éclairs. Dip the choux puff in syrup and set it on top of the circle.

Put the remaining Chantilly cream in a pastry bag fitted with a medium star tube and decorate between the éclairs and pastry ring and puff with rosettes of whipped cream.

Gâteau Alexandra

$\frac{1}{2}$ cup potato starch
3 tablespoons flour
$\frac{1}{2}$ cup sugar
$\frac{3}{4}$ cup whole blanched almonds, ground
4 eggs
$3\frac{1}{2}$ squares ($3\frac{1}{2}$ oz) semisweet chocolate, chopped
5 tablespoons butter
$\frac{1}{2}$ cup apricot jam glaze
2 cup quantity fondant icing, flavored with $1\frac{1}{2}$ squares ($1\frac{1}{2}$ oz) melted semisweet chocolate

8 inch square cake pan

Method
Set the oven at moderate (350°F), line pan with a square of wax paper and grease it.

Sift the flour with the potato starch. Put the sugar, ground almonds, 1 whole egg and 3 egg yolks in a bowl and beat until thick and light colored. Alternatively, work the mixture in a blender. Melt the chocolate on a heatproof plate over a pan of hot water, then let cool and beat into the egg mixture.

Warm the butter in a bowl or pan over hot water until it is very soft and pourable, taking care it does not become

too hot or oily. Stiffly whip the 3 egg whites.

Fold the flour into the chocolate mixture in 2–3 batches alternately with the egg whites. When the last batch of flour and whites are almost folded in, add the butter and fold in. Pour cake batter into the prepared pan and bake in heated oven for 30–35 minutes or until a skewer inserted in the center comes out clean. Turn the cake onto a wire rack to cool, then brush with apricot jam glaze and coat with chocolate fondant icing.

Note: for gâteau and pastry basic recipes, fillings and decorations, see pages 52–53.

Quantity Terms

Terms like 1 cup quantity pastry or 1 cup quantity butter cream frosting refer to the amount obtained by using 1 cup of the principal ingredient at the top of the ingredient list, not 1 cup of prepared pastry dough or butter cream frosting.

Tartelettes Perlées
(Pearled Tartlets)

1 cup quantity French flan
    pastry or pastry trimmings
1 cup quantity almond mousse
    filling (see gâteau Alcazar on
    page 56)
confectioners' sugar
    (for sprinkling)
$\frac{1}{4}$ cup apricot jam glaze
$\frac{1}{2}$ quantity of meringue
    Italienne (see page 53)

*Pastry bag; fine writing tube;
10–12 small tartlet pans*

Makes 10–12 tartlets.

Method
Set the oven at moderately
hot (375°F).
Chill the pastry dough 30
minutes. Roll it out thinly, line
the tartlet pans and prick the
bottoms. Fill tartlets with
almond mousse level with the
tops, sprinkle with confectioners' sugar and bake in
heated oven for 12–15 minutes or until firm in the center
and lightly browned. Remove
from pans and transfer to a
wire rack to cool completely.
Meanwhile make meringue
Italienne and put into the
pastry bag fitted with the
writing tube. Replace the
tartlets in the pans. Brush with
melted apricot jam glaze, let
set, then pipe a very fine
lattice of meringue on top and
surround the edge with dots
like 'pearls' (hence the name of
the pastries). Bake the tartlets
for 2–3 minutes longer in
heated oven to set the
meringue without browning.

Barquettes Italiennes
(Italian Boats)

1 cup quantity French flan
    pastry or pastry trimmings
1 cup quantity almond mousse
    filling (see gâteau Alcazar on
    page 56)
2 egg white quantity meringue
    Italienne (see page 53)
confectioners' sugar
    (for sprinkling)
1 tablespoon apricot jam glaze

*10–12 boat molds; pastry bag;
$\frac{1}{4}$ inch plain tube; paper
decorating cone*

Makes 10–12 boats.

Method
Chill pastry dough 30 minutes.
Set oven at moderately hot
(375°F).
Roll out dough, line the
molds, prick the bottom of
each mold and fill with almond
mousse level with the top.
Bake in heated oven for 10–12
minutes until lightly browned,
then turn upside down on a
wire rack to cool. Lower the
oven heat to moderately low
(325°F).
Meanwhile make the
meringue Italienne. Turn the
boats right side up and
replace in the molds. Cover
the tops with meringue, shap-
ing it to an inverted 'V' with a
knife. Put remaining meringue
in the pastry bag fitted with
the plain tube and pipe a scroll
on each boat. Sprinkle with
confectioners' sugar and bake
in heated oven for 3–5 minutes or until meringue tops are
very lightly browned. Let cool.
Put the apricot jam glaze in
the paper cone, snip off the
top and pipe a very thin line
of glaze along the top of each
scroll to emphasize it.

Duchesses Pralinées
(Praline Cookies)

$\frac{1}{4}$ cup flour
scant 1 cup sugar
$\frac{1}{4}$ cup whole blanched almonds,
    ground
$\frac{1}{4}$ cup shelled hazelnuts,
    browned and ground
3 egg whites
2 tablespoons melted butter
$\frac{1}{3}$ cup quantity butter cream
    frosting, flavored with 2–3
    teaspoons dry instant coffee

Pastry bag; medium star tube

Makes 18–22 cookies.

Method
Set oven at low (300°F).
Butter and flour a baking
sheet.
Mix flour, sugar and ground
nuts together. Stiffly whip egg
whites and fold in nut mixture with melted butter.
Spread mixture in ovals about
$2\frac{1}{2}$ inches long on prepared
baking sheet, leaving room for
the mixture to spread, and
bake in heated oven for 25–
30 minutes or until golden.
Transfer to a wire rack to cool.
Put frosting into the pastry
bag fitted with the star tube,
pipe frosting onto half the
cookies and place the remaining cookies on top.

**To brown and grind
hazelnuts:** bake in a
moderately hot oven
(375°F) for 8–10 min-
utes, then rub briskly in a
rough cloth to remove the
dry skins. Grind hazelnuts
in a rotary cheese grater
or work a few at a time in
a blender.

Petits Japonais
(Almond Meringue Cakes)

1 cup Japonais mixture (made
    with 1 cup ground almonds,
    1 cup sugar and 4 egg
    whites) – see box on page 58
$\frac{1}{2}$ cup quantity butter cream
    frosting 2, flavored with
    $\frac{1}{2}$ teaspoon vanilla

For white praline
$\frac{1}{2}$ cup sugar
$\frac{1}{2}$ cup water
$\frac{1}{2}$ cup whole blanched almonds,
    ground

Pastry bag; $\frac{1}{4}$ inch plain tube

Makes 12 petits Japonais.

Method
Set the oven at low (275°F)
and line a baking sheet with
silicone paper. Make the
Japonais mixture and put it
in the pastry bag fitted with
the plain tube. Pipe 2 inch
rounds in a spiral on the lined
baking sheet. Bake in heated
oven for 35–40 minutes until
the cakes are crisp and just
beginning to brown. Let cool to
tepid, peel off the paper and
transfer to a wire rack to cool
completely.
To make white praline: in a
saucepan heat the sugar with
the water until dissolved,
bring to a boil and boil until
the syrup forms a firm,
pliable ball when dropped in
cold water (250°F on a sugar
thermometer). Take from the
heat, add the ground almonds
and stir until the mixture is
cool and sandy in texture.
Work through a coarse sieve.
Flavor the butter cream
frosting with the vanilla.
Sandwich 2 cake rounds
together with frosting and
also spread the top and sides
with frosting. Coat each cake
with white praline, pressing it

Selection of French pastries (from left): tartelettes perlées; barquettes Italiennes; duchesse pralinées and petits Japonais

on with a metal spatula, and mark a lattice on top with the point of a knife.

Quantity Terms

Terms like 1 cup quantity pastry or 1 cup quantity butter cream frosting refer to the amount obtained by using 1 cup of the principal ingredient at the top of the ingredient list, not 1 cup of prepared pastry dough or butter cream frosting.

Financières

5 tablespoons butter
$\frac{1}{2}$ cup whole blanched almonds, ground
$\frac{1}{4}$ cup sugar
2 tablespoons potato starch
1 egg, beaten to mix
$\frac{1}{3}$ cup mixed candied fruits, finely chopped and macerated in 1 tablespoon rum
$\frac{1}{4}$ cup apricot jam glaze
1 cup quantity rum-flavored fondant icing
6 candied cherries, halved

10 boat molds

Potato starch is available in specialty stores and some supermarkets. Makes 10 cakes.

Method
Set oven at moderate (350°F) and grease and flour the molds.

Cream the butter and stir in the almonds, sugar, potato starch and egg. Stir in the macerated candied fruits.

Fill the molds with the butter mixture level to the top and bake in the heated oven for 7–10 minutes or until risen and browned. Cool them on a wire rack. Brush the tops with apricot jam glaze and let it set.

Melt the fondant icing and coat each cake with fondant, trimming the edges with the blade of a knife to give a neat finish. Top each cake with a halved candied cherry.

Tom Pouce (Tom Thumb)

1 cup quantity French flan pastry

For filling
6 tablespoons butter
6 tablespoons sugar
$\frac{3}{4}$ cup ground almonds
1–2 tablespoons water
1 tablespoon dry instant coffee
1 cup quantity coffee-flavored fondant or glacé icing
6 whole almonds, blanched, browned and split in half, lengthwise

Makes 12 cookies.

Method
Make the pastry dough and chill it 1 hour. Set oven at moderately hot (375°F).

Roll out the pastry dough $\frac{1}{4}$ inch thick and cut it into 24 2-inch squares. Set the squares on a baking sheet and bake in the heated oven for 8–10 minutes or until they are pale golden. Cool them on a wire rack.

To prepare the filling: cream the butter, gradually add the sugar and beat until soft and light. Work in the ground almonds with the instant coffee and enough water to make a soft paste.

Melt the fondant icing or make the glacé icing and flavor to taste with instant coffee; spread the icing over 12 pastry squares and let set. Spread the coffee almond filling on the other squares and place the iced squares on top.

Florettes

1 cup quantity French flan
   pastry
2–3 tablespoons apricot jam

For filling
2 small egg whites
6 tablespoons confectioners'
   sugar, sifted
½ cup whole blanched almonds,
   ground
2 teaspoons kirsch or
   ½ teaspoon almond extract
   (for flavoring)

To finish
¼ cup whole blanched
   almonds, coarsely chopped
confectioners' sugar
   (for sprinkling)

10–12 tartlet pans

Makes 10–12 tartlets.

Method
Make the pastry dough and
chill it. Set the oven at
moderately hot (375°F).

Roll out and line the tartlet
pans with pastry dough and
place a little apricot jam in
each one.

To make the filling: beat the
egg whites until they hold a
stiff peak, then fold in the
confectioners' sugar and
ground almonds with the
kirsch or almond extract.

Fill the mixture into the
tartlet molds and sprinkle the
tops with coarsely chopped
almonds. Sprinkle them
generously with confectioners'
sugar and bake in the heated
oven for about 15 minutes or
until the florettes are lightly
browned. Transfer to a wine
rack to cool.

Gâteaux Rivoli

4 egg quantity Génoise sponge
   cake batter
2 cups apricot jam glaze
1½ cups sugar cubes
confectioners' sugar
   (for sprinkling)

8 inch square cake pan

Makes 16 cakes.

Method
Set the oven at moderate
(350°F) and prepare the cake
pan as in the basic Génoise
recipe.

Make and bake the Génoise
sponge cake and turn out on
a wire rack to cool. Crush or
pound the cube sugar with a
rolling pin until it resembles
coarse crumbs.

Split the cake, sandwich it
with a little apricot jam glaze,
reshape it, trim the edges and
cut it into 2-inch squares.

Boil the remaining apricot
jam glaze until it is very thick.
Spear each cake through the
bottom with a two-pronged
fork and dip it in the hot glaze.
Spread it evenly with a metal
spatula and roll each cake in
crushed cube sugar. Sprinkle
the tops thickly with confectioners' sugar.

Heat several metal skewers
in a gas flame or under a
broiler until they are red hot
and mark a cross on the top of
each cake.

Lisettes

1 cup quantity French flan
   pastry
2 tablespoons apricot jam
3 egg whites
¼ cup sugar
½ cup whole blanched almonds,
   ground
piece of candied orange peel,
   cut in 12 small diamonds
confectioners' sugar (for
   sprinkling)

*12 boat molds (if possible with
   fluted edges)*

Makes 12 cakes.

Method
Make the pastry dough and
chill it 1 hour. Set the oven at
moderate (350°F).

Roll out the pastry dough
and line it into the molds; put
a teaspoon of apricot jam in
each one.

Beat the egg whites until
they hold a stiff peak, then
fold in the sugar and ground
almonds. Fill each pastry case
with almond mixture, add a
diamond of candied peel in
the center and sprinkle generously with confectioners'
sugar. Bake in the heated
oven for 12–15 minutes or
until the cakes are lightly
browned. Cool to tepid in the
molds before turning out
onto a wire rack.

Bateaux Bruxellois

1 cup quantity French flan
   pastry
¾ cup quantity pastry cream,
   flavored with a little vanilla
   or almond extract
½ cup whole blanched almonds,
   ground

For decoration
6 candied cherries
candied angelica, cut into
   24 small diamonds (optional)
confectioners' sugar
   (for sprinkling)

12 boat molds

Makes 12 boats.

Method
Make the pastry dough and
chill it 1 hour. Make the pastry
cream, cool it, then fold in the
ground almonds. Set the oven
at moderately hot (375°F).

Roll out and line the molds
with pastry dough and fill
them with the pastry cream
mixture, piling it high, shape
it to an inverted 'V' with the
blade of a knife.

Decorate each boat with
half a candied cherry and two
diamonds of angelica. Sprinkle
with confectioners' sugar and
bake the boats in the heated
oven for 10–12 minutes or
until they are lightly browned.
Transfer to a wire rack to cool.

Quantity Terms

Terms like 1 cup quantity
pastry or 1 cup quantity
butter cream frosting refer
to the amount obtained by
using 1 cup of the prin-
cipal ingredient at the top
of the ingredient list, not
1 cup of prepared pastry
dough or butter cream
frosting.

Pastry Cream

1½ cups milk
1 egg, separated
1 egg yolk
¼ cup sugar
1½ tablespoons flour
1 tablespoon cornstarch
vanilla bean (to flavor) or
  1–2 drops of vanilla
  extract, or 1–2 drops of
  almond extract, if using

Method
Beat the egg yolks with the sugar until thick and light. Stir in the flour and cornstarch and just enough cold milk to make a smooth paste. Add vanilla bean to remaining milk and scald. Cover and let stand 10–15 minutes to infuse.

Stir the hot milk into the egg mixture, blend, return to the pan and stir over gentle heat until boiling. **Watchpoint:** make sure cream is smooth before letting it boil. If lumps form as it thickens, take pan from heat and beat until smooth. Do not bring to a boil too quickly or the mixture may curdle before it thickens.

Cook the cream gently for 2 minutes, stirring; if it is too stiff, add a little more milk. Remove the vanilla bean. At this point, add the vanilla or almond extract, if using.

Beat the egg white until it holds a stiff peak and fold in a little of the hot pastry cream. Fold this mixture into the remaining hot cream and pour into a bowl. Let cool.

Mokatines

4 egg quantity Génoise sponge
  cake batter
¾ cup quantity coffee-flavored
  butter cream frosting 1
½ cup apricot jam glaze
2 cup quantity coffee flavored
  fondant icing

*8 inch square cake pan; pastry
bag and small star tube*

Makes 24 mokatines.

Method
Set the oven at moderate (350°F) and grease and flour the cake pan.

Make and bake the Génoise sponge cake and turn onto a wire rack to cool.

Make the coffee butter cream frosting.

When the cake is cool, split it and sandwich it with about one-third of the butter cream frosting. Reshape it, trim the sides and cut it into neat rectangles about 2¾ inches long and 1 inch wide. Brush the top and sides with melted apricot jam glaze and let set.

Melt the fondant icing and flavor it to taste with dry instant coffee. Coat each square with fondant icing and let set.

Put the butter cream frosting into the pastry bag fitted with a small star tube and pipe rosettes of frosting on top of each square.

AUSTRIAN

Kaisertorte
(Emperor's Cake)

For Japonais meringue base
1 cup whole blanched almonds,
  browned and ground
¾ cup sugar
3 egg whites

For cake
3 egg quantity Génoise sponge
  cake batter
grated rind of 1 lemon

To finish
1½ cup quantity butter cream
  frosting 1, flavored with
  1 tablespoon vanilla
yellow food coloring
½ cup raspberry jelly
1 cup quantity fondant icing,
  flavored with juice of ½ lemon
½ cup shredded almonds

*8–9 inch moule à manqué or
8 inch springform pan; pastry
bag; medium star tube*

Method
For Japonais base; line a baking sheet with silicone paper and mark an 11 inch circle on it. Set oven at low (300°F).

Make Japonais meringue mixture (see page 58), spread it on the prepared baking sheet on the marked circle and bake in heated oven for 35–40 minutes or until the Japonais is crisp and lightly browned. Let cool slightly, then carefully peel off the paper; transfer Japonais to a wire rack to cool completely.

Make Génoise cake batter, flavoring it with grated lemon rind instead of vanilla. Bake and turn onto a wire rack to cool. Make the vanilla butter cream frosting and add just enough food coloring to tint

it a pale yellow.

Melt the raspberry jelly over low heat, stirring until smooth. Split the cake, sandwich with raspberry jelly and brush the top with jelly. Spread the remaining jelly on the Japonais round, leaving a 1½ inch border and set the cake on top. Ice the top of the cake with fondant icing, flavored with the lemon juice. When set, spread the sides with butter cream frosting and press on shredded almonds with a metal spatula.

Put the remaining frosting into the pastry bag fitted with the star tube and decorate the top and around base of the cake with rosettes.

For kaisertorte, spread raspberry jelly on Japonais round, leaving 1½ inch border

Spread the sides of the cake with butter cream frosting and press on shredded almonds

The finished kaisertorte (recipe is on page 65)

66

Nusstorte
(Walnut Cake)

1 cup coarsely chopped
   walnuts, ground
½ cup dry white breadcrumbs
6 eggs, separated
1 cup sugar
1 tablespoon rum

For frosting
3 eggs
1 cup sifted confectioners'
   sugar
1 tablespoon rum
1¾ cups unsalted butter
1 cup chopped walnuts
caramelized walnuts (for
   decoration)

Two 9 inch cake pans

Method
Grease the pans, line each with a circle of wax paper, grease the paper and sprinkle the pans with flour, discarding the excess. Set the oven at moderate (350°F).

Sift the breadcrumbs through a coarse sieve. Beat the egg yolks with ½ cup sugar until thick and light, then beat in the ground walnuts and rum. Stiffly whip the egg whites, gradually beat in remaining sugar and continue beating until this meringue is stiff and glossy. Fold the breadcrumbs and meringue alternately into the walnut mixture as lightly as possible. Pour the mixture into the prepared pans and bake in heated oven for 20–25 minutes or until the tops spring back when lightly pressed with a fingertip. Turn out onto a wire rack to cool completely.

To make frosting: in a bowl beat the eggs until mixed, then gradually beat in the confectioners' sugar. Set the bowl over a pan of hot water and beat until the mixture is thick and stands in soft peaks. Take from heat, add rum and continue beating until the mixture is cool. If using an electric beater, no heat is necessary.

Cream the butter and beat it into the rum mixture with the chopped walnuts.

Sandwich the cakes with the frosting, and coat the top and sides thickly with frosting, roughening the surface. Decorate the top with caramelized walnuts. Chill before serving.

Caramelized Walnuts

Put ¼ cup sugar with ¾ cup water in a pan and bring to a boil. Add 1 tablespoon butter and boil syrup rapidly until mixture is caramel-colored. Dip bottom of pan in cold water to stop cooking and drop in about 12 walnut halves. Turn them gently so they are coated with caramel, then lift out onto an oiled plate and leave about 10 minutes to set.

Sachertorte
(Chocolate Cake)

7 squares (7 oz) semisweet
   chocolate, chopped
1 cup flour
pinch of salt
¾ cup butter
¾ cup sugar
8 eggs, separated
⅓ cup apricot jam glaze

For icing
1 cup cocoa, sifted
pinch of salt
⅔ cup heavy cream
1⅓ cups sugar
⅓ cup unsalted butter
1 teaspoon vanilla

*8 inch springform pan; paper
decorating cone*

Method
Grease the springform pan, line the base with a circle of wax paper, grease it and sprinkle the pan with flour, discarding the excess. Set the oven at moderate (350°F).

Sift the flour twice with the salt. Melt the chocolate on a heatproof plate over a pan of hot water and let cool. Cream the butter, gradually beat in the sugar and continue beating until soft and light. Beat in the egg yolks one by one, then beat in the cool but still soft chocolate, reserving about 1 tablespoon of chocolate for the final piping. Stiffly whip the egg whites and fold them in 2–3 batches into the chocolate mixture alternately with the flour. Pour into the prepared pan and bake in heated oven for 60–70 minutes or until a skewer inserted in the center comes out clean. Cool slightly, then turn onto a wire rack to cool completely. Brush the cake with melted apricot jam glaze and let set.

To make the icing: in a saucepan mix the cocoa, salt, cream, sugar and butter. Stir over low heat until the icing is melted and smooth. Stir in the vanilla and let cool until warm – it should have the consistency to coat the back of a spoon. If too thick, add a little more cream.

Pour the icing over the cake, spreading it quickly with a metal spatula. Mark the top into 6–8 wedges. Put the reserved melted chocolate into a paper decorating cone, snip off the end so it pipes in a thin line and write 'Sacher' along each wedge, starting with a large 'S' at the edge and working towards the center.

Quantity Terms

Terms like 1 cup quantity pastry or 1 cup quantity butter cream frosting refer to the amount obtained by using 1 cup of the principal ingredient at the top of the ingredient list, not 1 cup of prepared pastry dough or butter cream frosting.

Hazelnuss Küchlein
(Hazelnut Cookies)

1½ cups shelled hazelnuts, browned and ground (see box on page 62)
½ cup butter
½ cup sugar
1 cup flour

To finish
¼ cup raspberry jam
confectioners' sugar (for sprinkling)

3 inch and 1 inch cookie cutters

Makes 15–18 cookies.

Method
Set the oven at moderate (350°F) and grease a baking sheet.

Cream the butter, gradually beat in the sugar and continue beating until soft and light. Work in the ground hazelnuts and flour to make a smooth dough, cover tightly and chill 30 minutes. On a floured board, roll out the dough to ¼ inch thickness and stamp out 3 inch rounds. Stamp a 1 inch circle from the center of half of them. Set the rounds on the prepared baking sheet and bake in heated oven for 15–18 minutes or until beginning to brown around the edges. Transfer to a wire rack to cool.

Spread the whole rounds with raspberry jam and set rounds with center stamped out on top. Sprinkle the cookies generously with confectioners' sugar and pile a little more raspberry jam in the center of each one.

Vanillekipfeln
(Vanilla Crescents)

½ cup vanilla sugar (to finish)
¾ cup unsalted butter
⅓ cup sugar
1¼ cups flour
pinch of salt
1 cup whole blanched almonds, ground

Makes 28–30 crescents.

Method
Grease and flour a baking sheet and set oven at moderately low (325°F).

Cream the butter, gradually beat in the sugar and continue beating until soft and light. Sift the flour and salt, stir in ground almonds and work to a smooth dough. Wrap tightly and chill at least 30 minutes.

Divide dough into small balls, each about 1 tablespoon, and shape into rolls about 3 inches long. Curve into crescents and set on the prepared baking sheet. Bake in heated oven for 20–25 minutes or until lightly browned. While still hot, roll the crescents in vanilla sugar, then let cool.

Vanilla sugar (made by leaving a vanilla bean in a jar of sugar for several days or longer) can be used in any recipe instead of plain sugar and vanilla extract.

GERMAN

Schwarzwalder Kirschtorte
(Black Forest Cake)

¾ cup flour
2 teaspoons baking powder
1½ cups fresh breadcrumbs, made from dark rye bread
¾ cup slivered almonds, browned and ground
1½ squares (1½ oz) semisweet chocolate, finely grated
2 tablespoons cocoa
9 tablespoons butter
¾ cup sugar
5 eggs
2 tablespoons rum

For filling
¼ cup kirsch
1 cup black cherry preserve
Chantilly cream (made with 2 cups heavy cream, stiffly whipped and flavored with 2 tablespoons sugar and 2 teaspoons vanilla)
chocolate caraque

8 inch springform pan

Method
Sift the flour with the baking powder and mix with the dark rye breadcrumbs, ground almonds, grated chocolate and cocoa.

Set oven at moderate (350°F) and grease the springform pan.

In a bowl cream the butter, gradually beat in the sugar and continue beating until the mixture is soft and light. Beat in the eggs, one at a time, beating well after each addition. Fold in the flour and chocolate mixture in 3 portions, adding the rum with the last portion. Spoon the batter into the prepared pan and bake in heated oven for 40–50 minutes or until a

skewer inserted in the center of the cake comes out clean. Let cool in the pan for 5 minutes, then turn out and cool completely on a wire rack.

Split the cake in 3 layers and sprinkle each one with the kirsch. Spread 2 layers with cherry preserve, then with one-third of the Chantilly cream. Reshape the cake. Spread the remaining Chantilly cream over the top and sides and press on the chocolate caraque. Serve within 3–4 hours.

Shave off long scrolls of chocolate caraque

Chocolate Caraque

Melt 3 squares (3 oz) semisweet chocolate, grated or chopped, on a heatproof plate over a pan of hot water. Work with a metal spatula until the chocolate is smooth and spread it thinly on a marble slab or Formica-type surface. Leave until it is nearly set.

Hold a sharp, long knife almost at a right angle to the chocolate surface; shave off long chocolate scrolls or flakes using a slight sideways sawing movement.

Caraque looks better when fresh but can be kept a day or two in an airtight container.

SPANISH

Brazo de Gitano
(Gipsy's Arm Cake)

½ cup flour
pinch of salt
4 eggs, separated
½ cup sugar

For filling
1½ cups milk
1 vanilla bean, split
3 egg yolks
3 tablespoons sugar
2 tablespoons cornstarch
¼ cup dark rum
confectioners' sugar (for
 sprinkling)

11 X 15 inch jelly roll pan

This recipe was first given in Volume 16.

Method

Set oven at moderate (350°F). Grease the jelly roll pan, line the base with a rectangle of wax paper, grease it and sprinkle the pan with sugar, then with flour and discard excess.

To make jelly roll: sift the flour with the salt. Beat the egg yolks with the sugar until thick and light. Stiffly whip the egg whites and fold into the yolk mixture alternately with the sifted flour. Spread the batter in the prepared pan and bake in the heated oven for 12–15 minutes or until the edges are lightly browned.

Turn out jelly roll onto a dish towel or sheet of wax paper sprinkled with confectioners' sugar. Quickly but carefully remove the rectangle of wax paper, trim the edges of the cake to give a neat finish and remove the browned edges, and roll up tightly with the towel or wax paper inside;

let cool.

To make the filling: scald the milk with the vanilla bean, cover the pan and let stand in a warm place to infuse for 10 minutes. Beat the egg yolks with the sugar until slightly thickened and stir in the cornstarch. Strain in the hot milk, stir well and return to the pan. Bring to a boil, stirring until thickened, and simmer 2 minutes. Take from the heat, cover and let cool; beat in the rum.

Carefully unroll the jelly roll and remove the towel or paper. Spread the inside with the rum-flavored pastry cream, roll up the cake and sprinkle with confectioners' sugar.

Quantity Terms

Terms like 1 cup quantity pastry or 1 cup quantity butter cream frosting refer to the amount obtained by using 1 cup of the principal ingredient at the top of the ingredient list, not 1 cup of prepared pastry dough or butter cream frosting.

Note: for gâteau and pastry basic recipes, fillings and decorations, see pages 52–53.

For gipsy's arm cake, carefully tear the paper away from the jelly roll

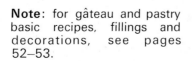

Trim the sides of the jelly roll with a knife to give a neat edge, then roll it up

HUNGARIAN

Doboz Torte
(Chocolate and Caramel Torte)

$1\frac{1}{4}$ cups flour
pinch of salt
4 eggs
$\frac{3}{4}$ cup sugar
$\frac{3}{4}$ cup quantity butter cream
    frosting 1, flavored with
    4 squares (4 oz) semisweet
    chocolate, melted and cooled

For caramel
$\frac{2}{3}$ cup sugar
$\frac{2}{3}$ cup water

Pastry bag; medium star tube

Method
Grease and flour 2–3 baking sheets and mark each with an 8 inch circle. Set the oven at moderately hot (375°F).

Sift the flour with the salt. Break the eggs into a bowl and gradually beat in the sugar. Set the bowl over a pan of hot water and beat until the mixture is light and thick enough to leave a ribbon trail on itself when the whisk is lifted. Take the bowl from the heat and continue beating until the mixture is cool. If using an electric beater, no heat is necessary. Fold the flour into mixture with a metal spoon.

Spoon one-sixth of the mixture onto each baking sheet and spread to about 8 inch circles. Bake in heated oven for 5–6 minutes or until very lightly browned. While the mixture is still warm trim neatly with a knife to 8 inch rounds and transfer them to a wire rack to cool. Cool the baking sheets, grease and flour them again and continue baking the remaining mixture.

Set 1 round on an oiled baking sheet, ready to coat with caramel.

To make the caramel: melt sugar in the water over low heat, then bring to a boil and boil steadily to a rich brown caramel. Stop it cooking by dipping the base of the pan in cold water, let the bubbles in the caramel subside and pour it over a single round. When the caramel is on the point of setting, mark it into 6–8 wedges with the back of a knife and trim the edges. This will be the top of the 'torte'. When cold, crush the caramel trimmed from the edges and reserve for decoration.

Sandwich the cake layers with some of the frosting, setting the caramel-covered round on top, then spread the sides with more frosting, reserving $\frac{1}{4}$ cup for decoration. Press the crushed caramel around the sides. Put the reserved frosting in the pastry bag fitted with the star tube and pipe rosettes of frosting around the top of the cake.

For doboz torte, coat cake round with caramel and, when on the point of setting, mark it in wedges with the back of a knife

Note: for gâteau and pastry basic recipes, fillings and decorations, see pages 52–53.

SWISS

Basler Leckerli
(Honey Cookies)

1 cup honey
1 cup sugar
1 cup slivered almonds
grated rind of $\frac{1}{2}$ lemon
$\frac{1}{4}$ cup chopped candied orange
    peel
$\frac{1}{4}$ cup chopped candied lemon
    peel
1 teaspoon ground cinnamon
$\frac{1}{2}$ teaspoon ground cloves
$\frac{1}{4}$ teaspoon ground nutmeg
1 tablespoon kirsch
3 cups flour

For glaze
$\frac{1}{2}$ cup sugar
$\frac{1}{4}$ cup water

*Leckerli or springerle mold
(optional)*

Method
In a saucepan bring honey to a boil, stir in sugar off the heat, and heat gently until sugar dissolves. Stir in almonds, grated lemon rind, candied peel and spices. Heat the kirsch in a ladle, flame it and add to the almond mixture.

Take from the heat and gradually add the flour. As soon as the dough is cool enough to handle, work it with your hands until smooth. Let stand 1 hour in a warm place so the dough remains pliable, then roll out on a floured board to $\frac{1}{4}$ inch thickness and cut into pieces the size of the mold. Sprinkle the mold with flour and remove excess. Press the pieces of dough firmly into the mold or roll them on the mold with a rolling pin so the design is clearly impressed. If not using molds, cut dough into $1\frac{1}{2}$ X $1\frac{1}{2}$

inch rectangles. Place close together on a greased, floured baking sheet, and let stand overnight to dry. Set the oven at moderately low (325°F) and bake the cookies 25–30 minutes or until golden brown.

For the glaze: heat sugar with water until dissolved, then boil until the syrup forms a thread between finger and thumb when a little is lifted on a spoon (230°F–234°F on a sugar thermometer). Brush syrup on the warm cookies. Cool, then pack cookies in an airtight container; store at least 4 weeks for honey flavor to mellow.

Leckerli cookies and their German cousin, **springerle** (see Volume 11) are traditionally shaped with wooden molds, carved with a wide variety of designs. The cookie dough is pressed into them before baking.

Doboz torte, sandwiched with chocolate butter cream frosting, is decorated with caramel and rosettes of chocolate frosting

Zuger Kirschtorte

3 egg quantity Génoise sponge
   cake batter

For Japonais meringue layers
1 cup blanched whole almonds,
   ground
$\frac{3}{4}$ cup sugar
3 egg whites

To finish
1 cup quantity butter cream
   frosting 2, flavored with 2
   tablespoons kirsch
3–4 tablespoons kirsch
   (for sprinkling)
confectioners' sugar
   (for sprinkling)
$\frac{1}{2}$ cup browned, slivered
   almonds, chopped

8 inch springform pan

This cake mellows if kept 12–
24 hours before serving.

Method
Mark 8-inch circles on 2
sheets of silicone paper. Set
the oven at low (300°F).

Make Japonais meringue
mixture (see page 58), spread
on prepared sheet in two
8-inch circles and bake in
heated oven for 25–30
minutes or until crisp and
very lightly browned. Trim the
rounds neatly with a knife
while still hot, let cool to
tepid, peel off paper and
transfer to a wire rack to
cool completely.

Make and bake the Génoise
sponge cake; turn out on a
wire rack to cool.

To assemble the cake:
spread a thin layer of the
frosting on 1 Japonais layer
and set the sponge cake on
top. Sprinkle the sponge cake
generously with kirsch. Spread
the remaining Japonais layer
with frosting and set it on
top of the cake, cream side
down. Coat the top and sides
of the cake with the remaining frosting and sprinkle the
top thickly with confectioners'
sugar. Press the slivered
almonds around sides.

DANISH

Prinsesstarta
(Princess Cake)

1 tablespoon flour
$\frac{1}{2}$ cup potato starch
5 eggs
$\frac{2}{3}$ cup sugar

For filling
1 envelope gelatin
$\frac{1}{4}$ cup water
$1\frac{1}{2}$ cups light cream
3 egg yolks
3 tablespoons sugar
2 teaspoons potato starch
1 cup heavy cream, whipped
   until it holds a soft shape
1 teaspoon vanilla

To finish
$4\frac{1}{2}$ cup quantity marzipan for
   decoration (see box)
green and yellow food coloring
confectioners' sugar (for
   sprinkling)

*9 inch moule à manqué or 10
   inch cake pan; 1 inch fluted
   cookie cutter; sugar
   thermometer*

Method
Grease the pan, line the base
with a circle of wax paper,
grease the paper and sprinkle
the pan with flour, discarding
the excess. Set the oven at
moderate (350°F).

Sift the flour with the $\frac{1}{2}$ cup
potato starch. In a bowl beat
the eggs until mixed and
gradually beat in the sugar.
Set the bowl over a pan of hot
water and beat until the mixture is thick and light and
leaves a trail on itself when
the beater is lifted. Take from
heat and beat until mixture is
cool. If using an electric
beater, no heat is necessary.

Fold flour mixture as lightly
as possible into egg mixture
in 2–3 batches. Pour cake
batter into the prepared pan;
bake in heated oven for 30–
35 minutes or until the top
springs back when lightly
pressed with a fingertip. Turn
onto a wire rack to cool
completely.

To make the filling: sprinkle
the gelatin over the water and
let stand 5 minutes until
spongy. Scald the cream.
Beat the egg yolks with the
sugar until slightly thickened,
then stir in the potato starch.
Stir in the hot cream, return
the mixture to the pan and
heat, stirring, until the cream
thickens. Simmer 2 minutes
and take from the heat. Stir
in gelatin until dissolved, then
cover cream and let cool.

When cold but not set, fold
in the whipped cream with the
vanilla. Split the cake and
sandwich with half the cream
mixture. Set the cake on a
platter, spread the remaining
cream over the top and sides
and chill 1–2 hours until the
cream is firmly set.

Color two-thirds of the marzipan a delicate green. On a
board sprinkled with confectioners' sugar, roll out the
green marzipan to an 11-inch
circle. Lift it onto the cake and
press down the sides so the
cake is completely covered
and the marzipan has no
wrinkles. Color 1 tablespoon
remaining marzipan bright
yellow.

Roll out remaining uncolored
marzipan very thinly and
stamp out 1-inch rounds
with the fluted cookie cutter.
Make a cut from the edge to
the center of each round and
overlap cut edges slightly to
form a flower shape.

Roll the yellow marzipan
into tiny balls and set a ball at
the center of each flower.
Sprinkle the top of the cake
lightly with confectioners'
sugar and arrange the flowers
in a border around the edge.

Marzipan for Decoration

For $4\frac{1}{2}$ cup quantity: in a
saucepan heat 2 cups
granulated sugar with 1
cup water until dissolved.
Bring to a boil and cook
steadily until the syrup
spins a thread when a
little is lifted on a spoon
(230°F–234°F on a
sugar thermometer). Take
pan from heat; beat until
the syrup looks slightly
cloudy.

Stir in $4\frac{1}{2}$ cups of
blanched ground
almonds, add 2 lightly
beaten egg whites and
cook over gentle heat
for 2–3 minutes or until
mixture pulls away from
sides of pan. Add the juice
of $\frac{1}{2}$ lemon and 1 teaspoon vanilla and turn the
mixture onto a board
sprinkled with 3–4 table-
spoons of confectioners'
sugar.

When the marzipan is
cool, knead it until
smooth.

ITALIAN

Torta d'Amatio

For almond pastry
1 cup flour
¾ cup whole blanched almonds, ground
grated rind of ½ lemon
⅓ cup butter, softened
⅓ cup sugar
2 egg yolks

For filling
1½ cup quantity pastry cream
   (see box on page 65)
5 tablespoons praline powder
   (see box on page 53)

To finish
1 egg white, beaten until frothy
sugar (for sprinkling)

8 inch flan ring

Method
Make pastry dough as for French flan pastry, adding the ground almonds and lemon rind to the flour. Chill for 30 minutes.

Make pastry cream, cover with plastic wrap and cool. Then stir in the praline powder.

Set oven at moderate (350°F). Roll out two-thirds of the dough and line the flan ring. Fill with the praline cream, roll out the remaining dough and cover the cream with it. Flute the edges to seal the pastry, brush the top with beaten egg white and sprinkle with sugar. Bake in heated oven for 30–35 minutes or until golden brown; transfer to a wire rack to cool completely.

Note: for gâteau and pastry basic recipes, fillings and decorations, see pages 52–53.

Cannoli
(Cream 'Pipes')

1½ cups flour
pinch of salt
2 tablespoons sugar
about 6 tablespoons Marsala
   or sherry
deep fat (for frying)

For filling
2 cups (1 lb) ricotta cheese
½ cup sugar
¼ cup mixed chopped candied
   fruit
¼ cup shelled pistachios,
   chopped
2 squares (2 oz) semisweet
   chocolate, chopped
1 teaspoon vanilla

To finish
¼ cup chopped pistachios or
   browned, chopped almonds
confectioners' sugar
   (for sprinkling)

*12–14 cannoli tubes; pastry
bag and ½ inch plain tube*

Cannoli, meaning 'pipes', are shaped around special 1 inch metal tubes. A good substitute can be made with a double thickness of heavy duty foil, or metal cornet molds may be used. If you prefer, the ricotta cheese can be flavored with sugar and ¼ cup Marsala instead of the candied fruits, pistachios, chocolate and vanilla. Makes 8–10 cannoli. This recipe was first given in Volume 8.

Method
To make the pastry dough: sift the flour with the salt into a bowl, add the sugar, make a well in the center, add the Marsala or sherry and work to a smooth, fairly stiff dough, adding more wine, if necessary. Knead the dough on a lightly floured board for 10 minutes or until very smooth and elastic; cover and chill for 2 hours.

Let the dough come to room temperature, then roll as thinly as possible on a floured board and cut in 5 inch squares. Wrap each square diagonally around a tube so a corner is at each end; moisten the central overlapping corner with water and press down firmly to seal the 'pipe', leaving both ends open.

Heat the deep fat to 375°F on a fat thermometer and lower in 3–4 cannoli at a time in a frying basket. Fry them until golden brown, lift out and drain on paper towels. Continue frying the remaining cannoli. When cool, slip them off the tubes.

To make the filling: work the cheese through a sieve, then beat it with the sugar until smooth and light. Beat in the candied fruit, pistachios, chopped chocolate and vanilla.

Put the filling into the pastry bag fitted with the plain tube and pipe the mixture into the cannoli shells to fill them. Dip each end into the chopped pistachios or almonds and sprinkle the pastry with confectioners' sugar.

Fave dei Morti
(Dead Men's Beans)

1 cup whole blanched almonds,
   ground
¾ cup flour
1 teaspoon ground cinnamon
¼ cup butter
¾ cup sugar
grated rind of 1 lemon
1 egg, beaten to mix

These small bean-shaped macaroons are made throughout Italy on All Soul's Day. Makes about 24 'beans'.

Method
Grease a baking sheet and set oven at moderate (350°F).

Work the ground almonds through a coarse sieve with the flour and cinnamon. Work in the butter with the fingertips until the mixture resembles crumbs, stir in the sugar and lemon rind and add the egg. Stir to mix, then work to form a smooth dough.

Roll the dough into balls the size of small walnuts, and shape them into ovals like beans. Set them on the prepared baking sheet and bake in heated oven for 15–20 minutes or until lightly browned. Transfer to a wire rack to cool completely.

Sole Lasserre — sole fillets are served in a pie pastry shell with mushrooms, asparagus and béchamel sauce (recipe is on page 77)

CLASSIC FISH DISHES

Fish, except for shellfish, tends to be forgotten when planning a party menu, yet there are many superb fish dishes that make delicious and unusual entrées. Don't be deterred if the fish called for in a specific recipe is not available because any similar type can be substituted. For example, small fresh flounder is an excellent substitute for sole.

More classic fish dishes were included in Volume 14.

Salmon with Fennel or Dill

10–12 lb whole salmon, with the head
3 quart quantity court bouillon (see box on page 82)

For garnish
1½ tablespoons chopped fresh fennel or dill
8 cucumbers, peeled, seeded and cut in sticks
¼ cup butter
salt and pepper

For butter sauce
1½ cups butter
4 shallots or 1 large onion, finely chopped
4 cups white wine
8 egg yolks, beaten to mix

For velouté sauce
⅓ cup butter
⅓ cup flour
5 cups chicken stock

To finish
1 cup heavy cream
2 tablespoons chopped fresh fennel or dill

Serves 10–12.

Method
Wash the salmon, trim the fins and cut the tail in a 'V'. Set salmon on the buttered rack of a fish kettle or wrap it tightly in cheesecloth and place in a roasting pan. Pour over the court bouillon, cover with the lid or foil and poach on top of the stove for 40–50 minutes or in a moderate oven (350°F) for 1 hour or until the fish flakes when tested with a fork.

To prepare the garnish: blanch the cucumber sticks in boiling water for 2–3 minutes and drain well. Return them to the pan with the butter and seasoning, cover and cook gently for 4–5 minutes or until just tender. Add fennel or dill

and keep warm.

To make the butter sauce: add the shallot or onion to the wine and reduce it by half. Beat the egg yolks in a bowl or in the top of a double boiler with 2 tablespoons butter until light and slightly thickened. Strain in the reduced wine, stirring, set over hot but not boiling water or in a water bath and gradually beat in the remaining butter, piece by piece; the sauce should thicken to the consistency of heavy cream. Taste for seasoning and reserve.

To make the velouté sauce: melt the butter, add the flour and cook to a pale straw color. Cool a little and stir in the chicken stock, off the heat. Bring to a boil, stirring, and simmer 5 minutes or until it is the consistency of heavy cream. Cool a little, then gradually beat in the butter sauce, off the heat. Add the cream and fennel or dill, taste for seasoning and keep warm in a water bath.
Watchpoint: the sauce will curdle if it gets too hot.

When the fish is cooked, drain it and remove the cheesecloth, if necessary. Peel off the skin, leaving the head and tail, and remove the small bones along the back. Set the fish on a platter, spoon over enough sauce to coat it and serve the rest separately. Garnish the dish with cucumber and herb mixture.

Timbale à l'Indienne is filled with a curried shrimp mixture

Timbale à l'Indienne
(Curried Shrimp Pie)

rich pie pastry (made with 1 cup flour, ¼ teaspoon salt, 3 tablespoons butter, 3 tablespoons shortening, 1 egg yolk, 1–2 tablespoons cold water)
paprika (for sprinkling)

For curry sauce
1 tablespoon curry powder
2 tablespoons butter
2 small onions, finely chopped
béchamel sauce, made with 2 tablespoons butter, 2 tablespoons flour, 2 cups milk (infused with slice of onion, 6 peppercorns, blade of mace and bay leaf)
2 tablespoons heavy cream
salt and pepper

For filling
3 hard-cooked eggs, quartered
¾ cup rice
1½ cups (½ lb) cooked, peeled shrimps

9 inch pie pan

Method
Boil the rice, drain, let dry and keep warm.

To make rich pie pastry dough: sift flour and salt into a bowl. Cut butter and shortening into the flour until in small pieces and well coated. Then rub in with the fingertips until the mixture looks like crumbs. Make a well in the center and add egg yolk and 1–2 tablespoons water and stir to combine. With a knife, quickly draw the flour into mixture in the center, adding more water if necessary to form a smooth dough.

Turn onto a floured board or marble slab and knead lightly until smooth. Wrap in wax paper, plastic wrap or bag. Chill the dough 30 minutes.

Set the oven at hot (400°F). Roll out the dough, line the pie pan and bake blind in heated oven for 10 minutes. Turn down the heat to moderately hot (375°F) and bake 10–12 minutes longer or until the pastry is browned. Take out and turn oven to low (300°F).

To make the curry sauce: melt the butter in a pan, add onion and cook gently until soft but not browned. Stir in the curry powder and cook gently 3–4 minutes longer. Add the béchamel sauce, simmer 2–3 minutes, then add cream and taste for seasoning.

Fill the pastry shell with the

eggs, cooked rice and shrimps in layers and spoon over the curry sauce. Heat in the low oven for 10–12 minutes or until very hot and sprinkle the top with paprika.

Timbale is a term used to describe dishes cooked or served in a pie crust. It may also be used to describe different types of metal, china or earthenware pans for cooking.

Sole Lasserre

1 lb sole fillets
rich pie pastry (made with
  $1\frac{1}{2}$ cups flour, pinch of salt,
  $\frac{1}{2}$ cup butter, 1 egg yolk and
  2–3 tablespoons cold water)
  – see method in timbale à
  l'Indienne
2 cups ($\frac{1}{2}$ lb) mushrooms
1 shallot, finely chopped
salt
$\frac{1}{2}$ cup white wine, or $\frac{1}{2}$ cup
  water and a squeeze of
  lemon juice
6 peppercorns
2 tablespoons butter
$\frac{3}{4}$ lb fresh asparagus, cooked
  and drained (see page 89),
  or 1 package frozen
  asparagus, cooked according
  to package directions
béchamel sauce, made with
  2 tablespoons butter,
  2 tablespoons flour, $1\frac{1}{4}$ cups
  milk (infused with slice of
  onion, 6 peppercorns, blade
  of mace and bay leaf)
1 egg yolk
2 tablespoons butter (to finish)

8 inch flan ring

Method

Chill pastry dough 30 minutes. Set oven at hot (400°F).

Roll out pastry dough, line flan ring and bake blind in heated oven for 10 minutes. Turn down heat to moderately hot (375°F) and bake 15 minutes longer or until the pastry is browned. Let pastry shell cool. Turn over to moderate (350°F).

Slice half the mushrooms; chop the rest. Cut each fillet of sole into 2–3 pieces and place it in a buttered baking dish with the shallot and sliced mushrooms. Sprinkle lightly with salt, pour over the wine or water and lemon juice and put the peppercorns at one side. Cover with buttered foil and poach in heated oven for 10–12 minutes or until the fish flakes when tested with a fork.

In a saucepan heat the 2 tablespoons butter, add the chopped mushrooms and cook 1–2 minutes until tender. Let cool, then spread in the bottom of the pastry shell and set it on a platter. Drain the fish and sliced mushrooms, reserving the liquid, and arrange in the pastry shell with the cooked asparagus spears.

Strain the cooking liquid into a saucepan and boil until reduced by half.

Make the béchamel sauce, and stir in the reduced cooking liquid. Take from the heat, beat in the egg yolk and stir in the remaining 2 tablespoons butter, a small piece at a time. Taste for seasoning, spoon the sauce over the fish to coat it completely and warm the pie in the heated oven for 5–6 minutes before serving.

Sole Suchet

$1\frac{1}{2}$ lb sole fillets
$\frac{1}{2}$ cup white wine
squeeze of lemon juice
2 medium carrots
$\frac{1}{2}$ tablespoon butter
$\frac{1}{4}$ cup Madeira or sherry
mousseline stuffing
béchamel sauce, made with
  $2\frac{1}{2}$ tablespoons butter,
  $2\frac{1}{2}$ tablespoons flour,
  $1\frac{1}{2}$ cups milk (infused with
  slice of onion,
  6 peppercorns, blade of
  mace and bay leaf)
2 tablespoons heavy cream
3–4 medium tomatoes,
  peeled and halved
salt and pepper
sugar
4–6 small mushrooms,
  sautéed until tender in
  1 tablespoon butter

Method

Make the mousseline stuffing. Make the béchamel sauce and keep warm. Set oven at moderate (350°F).

Wash and dry the sole fillets, flatten them slightly and spread the stuffing on the skinned sides. Fold them over, neaten the edges and lay the fillets in a lightly buttered baking dish. Pour over white wine and lemon juice, cover with buttered foil and poach in the heated oven for 15 minutes or until the fish flakes easily.

Cut the orange part of the carrots into julienne strips, discarding the hard yellow core, and put them in a small pan with $\frac{1}{2}$ tablespoon butter and the Madeira or sherry. Cover the pan tightly and simmer 6–7 minutes or until the carrots are tender.

When fish is cooked, drain the fillets on paper towels, strain the cooking liquid into the béchamel sauce and simmer until it is the consistency of heavy cream. Add the cream and carrots with their liquid. Season the tomatoes lightly with salt, pepper and sugar, and broil 4–5 inches from the heat, turning once, for 6–8 minutes, or until they are just cooked, or bake them in the heated oven.

Arrange the fillets of sole in a hot serving dish, coat with the sauce and top each fillet with a tomato half and a small mushroom. Serve with 'fish' potatoes.

Mousseline Stuffing

To fill $1\frac{1}{2}$ lb of fish fillets: wash and dry $\frac{1}{2}$ lb perch, whitefish or flounder fillet and remove any bones. Pass the fish twice through the fine blade of a grinder, then pound until smooth in a mortar and pestle and gradually work in 2 egg whites. Or, instead of pounding, work the fish with the egg whites for a few seconds in a blender until very smooth.

Gradually beat in $\frac{3}{4}$ cup heavy cream, then add seasoning.

'Fish' Potatoes

Peel 3 medium potatoes and quarter them lengthwise. Pare away sharp edges with a vegetable peeler and shape into ovals. Cook in a pan of boiling salted water for about 7 minutes, drain and return to the pan. Cover with foil and the lid; cook 4–5 minutes longer over very low heat or until tender. This prevents the potatoes from breaking and makes them dry and tender.

Sole with pineapple is served cold on a bed of potato salad and garnished with pineapple, tomato and chopped parsley

Sole aux Ananas
(Sole with Pineapple)

1½ lb sole fillets
¼ cup water
juice of ½ lemon
slice of onion
6 peppercorns
pinch of salt
6–8 small new potatoes
6 tablespoons vinaigrette
   dressing (see page 44)
1 fresh pineapple, peeled,
   cored and sliced, or 1 can
   (14 oz) pineapple slices,
   drained
squeeze of lemon juice
½ teaspoon paprika (optional)
1–2 tablespoons sugar
   (optional)
2 tomatoes, peeled, seeded and
   cut in strips
1 tablespoon chopped parsley

Method
Set oven at moderate (350°F).
   Fold the fillets of sole in three, place them in a buttered baking dish and add the water, lemon juice, slice of onion, peppercorns and a pinch of salt. Cover with buttered foil and bake in heated oven for 12–15 minutes or until the fish flakes easily; let cool in the liquid.
   Cook potatoes, unpeeled, in boiling salted water for 15–20 minutes or until just tender and drain them. Peel them while still hot, cut in thick slices and sprinkle with ¼ cup vinaigrette dressing.
   Sprinkle the pineapple with lemon juice, paprika if using, and a little sugar if the pineapple is fresh.
   Arrange the potato salad down the center of a platter, drain the sole fillets on paper towels and arrange on top of the potatoes. Overlap the pineapple slices around the dish. Mix the tomato strips with the remaining vinaigrette dressing and parsley and spoon them on top of the fish.

For sole with pineapple, peel cooked new potatoes while still hot, cut them in slices and sprinkle with vinaigrette dressing

Arrange fillets of sole on top of the potatoes before completing the dish

Red Snapper
Boulangere

1½–2 lb red snapper steaks
5–6 tablespoons butter
3–4 medium potatoes
15–18 small onions
1 teaspoon sugar
squeeze of lemon juice
1 tablespoon chopped parsley
   (for garnish)
salt

Method
Set oven at moderate (350°F).
   Wash and dry snapper steaks. Cut flesh from the bones in large chunks, removing any skin. Place the fish in an ovenproof dish, melt half the butter and pour it on top. Bake, basting often, in heated oven for 15 minutes or until the fish flakes easily when tested with a fork.
   Peel the potatoes, cut in quarters lengthwise and trim off the sharp edges. Blanch by putting in cold water, bringing to a boil and simmering 2 minutes; drain. Blanch, drain and peel onions. In a frying pan or skillet melt half the remaining butter, and cook the potatoes gently until golden and tender, turning them so they brown evenly. Remove and keep warm.
   Add onions to the pan with the remaining butter, sprinkle with the sugar and fry gently, shaking the pan so they brown evenly. When brown, cover the pan and cook for a few minutes longer or until the onions are tender.
   Set the fish down the center of the dish in which it was cooked, baste it with butter and juices, then spoon potatoes down one side and the onions down the other. Bake in heated oven 3–5 minutes longer, squeeze a little lemon juice over the fish and sprinkle with chopped parsley. Sprinkle potatoes with salt and serve.

Red Snapper
Mentonnaise

1½ lb red snapper fillets
¼ cup water
squeeze of lemon juice
slice of onion
6 peppercorns
salt
1 cup rice
¼ cup vinaigrette dressing
   (see page 44)
1 cup mayonnaise
   (see page 86)
1 teaspoon anchovy paste
   (or to taste)
few drops of red food coloring
   (optional)
8 anchovy fillets
2 tomatoes, peeled, seeded
   and cut in strips
½ cup ripe olives, pitted

Method
Set oven at moderate (350°F).
   Lay the fish fillets in a buttered baking dish, add water, lemon juice, onion, peppercorns and a pinch of salt. Cover with buttered foil and bake in heated oven for 12–15 minutes or until fish flakes easily; let cool in the liquid.
   Cook the rice in boiling, salted water for 12–15 minutes, drain it, rinse with cold water and spread out in an airy place to dry. Toss rice with 1 tablespoon vinaigrette dressing, stir in 1–2 tablespoons mayonnaise to bind mixture; pile it down center of a platter.
   Drain the fish on paper towels and arrange on top of the rice. Flavor the remaining mayonnaise with anchovy paste to taste, color it a delicate pink with a few drops of red food coloring, if you like, and thin it with hot water to a consistency to coat the back of a spoon. Coat fish with mayonnaise and decorate with an anchovy fillet.
   Mix tomatoes and olives with remaining dressing and arrange around the fish.

Flounder Mâconnaise

1½ lb flounder fillets
½ cup Mâcon wine or other
    red Burgundy
¼ cup water
6 peppercorns
bay leaf
slice of onion
salt
1½ tablespoons butter
10–12 small onions, blanched
    and peeled
1 teaspoon sugar
1 cup (¼ lb) mushrooms,
    trimmed
1 tablespoon water
squeeze of lemon juice

For sauce
2 tablespoons butter
1½ tablespoons flour
⅓ cup light cream

Method
Set oven at moderate (350°F).
    Fold each fish fillet in half.
Lay fillets in a buttered baking
dish, pour over the wine and
water and add the pepper-
corns, bay leaf, slice of onion
and a pinch of salt. Cover with
buttered foil and poach in the
heated oven for 12–15 minutes or until the fish flakes
easily when tested with a
fork.
    Melt 1 tablespoon butter in
a pan, add the blanched
onions, sprinkle them with
sugar, cover and cook gently,
shaking the pan occasionally
to prevent them from sticking,
for 10–12 minutes, or until
the onions are tender and
golden brown with caramel.
Put the mushrooms in a pan
with the water, remaining
butter and a squeeze of lemon
juice, cover and cook quickly
for 1–2 minutes or until just
tender. Keep mushrooms and
onions warm.
    Take out the fish, reserving
the cooking liquid. Drain fillets
on paper towels, arrange on
a platter and keep warm.
    To make the sauce: in a pan
melt the butter, stir in the
flour and cook until pale
straw-colored. Take from the
heat, strain in the cooking
liquid from the fish and bring
to a boil, stirring. Simmer
2–3 minutes, add the cream,
bring just back to a boil and
taste for seasoning.
    To serve, spoon sauce over
the fish and arrange mushrooms and onions around the
edge.

Flounder Véronique

1½–2 lb flounder fillets
½ cup water
½ cup white wine
6 peppercorns
slice of onion
½ lb seedless green grapes
squeeze of lemon juice
1 tablespoon chopped parsley

For sauce
3 tablespoons butter
2 tablespoons flour
1 egg yolk
½ cup light cream
salt and pepper
little sugar (optional)

Method
Wash and dry flounder fillets.
Cut them in half down the
center, fold the ends under
neatly and lay in a buttered
baking dish. Pour over the
water and wine and add
peppercorns and onion. Cover
with buttered paper and
poach in a moderate oven
(350°F) for 10–12 minutes or
until the fish just flakes easily
when tested with a fork. Drain
well on paper towels, arrange
on a platter and keep warm.
Strain cooking liquid and
reserve.
    Take grapes from the stems,
add a squeeze of lemon juice,
cover and reserve.
    To make the sauce: melt
butter in a saucepan, stir in
flour off the heat and add
reserved cooking liquid. Bring
to a boil, stirring, simmer 2
minutes and taste for seasoning. Mix together the egg
yolk and cream, add a little of
the hot sauce and stir this
liaison into the remaining
sauce. Heat, stirring, until
the sauce thickens slightly,
but do not boil or it may
curdle.
    Add the grapes to the
sauce, heat thoroughly, taste
for seasoning, adding a little
sugar if necessary to develop
the flavor of the grapes, and
spoon the sauce over the
fish. Sprinkle with chopped
parsley and serve.

Halibut Dieppoise

1½ lb halibut steaks
salt and pepper
juice of ½ lemon
¼ cup melted butter

For salpicon
3–4 leeks, washed
2 tablespoons butter
1 teaspoon paprika
1 cup (⅓ lb) cooked peeled
    shrimps
black pepper, freshly ground

Method
Set oven at moderate (350°F).
    Place the fish in a baking
dish, season and sprinkle with
the lemon juice. Pour over the
melted butter, cover with foil
and bake, basting occasionally, in heated oven for 15–20
minutes or until the fish flakes
easily.
    To make salpicon: slice the
white part of the leeks in
rounds and cut the green part
in julienne strips. Melt the
butter, add the white part of
the leek, press a piece of foil
on top, add the lid and cook
very gently (sweat) without
browning until soft. Add the
paprika and shrimps and heat
gently. Blanch the green part
of the leeks in boiling water
for 2–3 minutes, drain, refresh
and drain again. Add to pan
with shrimps and season well
with black pepper and a little
salt.
    Carefully drain fish pieces,
reserving the cooking liquid.
Remove bones and skin, keeping fish pieces as intact as
possible, and arrange them on
a platter. Spoon shrimp and
leek salpicon on top and
spoon over the strained cooking liquid.

Halibut with Cider

1½–2 lb halibut fillets
1 cup cider
½ cup water
2 tablespoons butter
1½ tablespoons flour
squeeze of lemon juice
1 tablespoon chopped parsley
2 tablespoons light cream
salt and pepper

Method
Set oven at moderate (350°F).
    Wash the fillets, dry and cut
into serving pieces. Lay pieces
in a buttered baking dish and
pour over the cider and water.
Cover with buttered foil and
poach in heated oven for
10–12 minutes or until fish
flakes easily when tested with
a fork. Transfer the fish to a
platter and keep warm; strain
the cooking liquid and reserve.
    In a saucepan melt butter,
stir in flour off the heat and
pour in reserved liquid. Bring
to a boil and simmer 3–4
minutes. Add lemon juice,
parsley and cream, taste for
seasoning and spoon over fish.

Classic fish dishes

Halibut Dieppoise is garnished with a shrimp and leek salpicon seasoned with a little paprika

Bass Caprice

1½–2 lb center cut piece of sea or striped bass
¼ cup seasoned flour (made with ¼ teaspoon salt and pinch of pepper)
2 tablespoons oil and 2 tablespoons butter (for frying)

For sauce and garnish
2 tablespoons fish stock (made with fish bone, ½ cup water, slice of onion and 3 peppercorns)
2 tablespoons butter
1 large carrot, cut in julienne strips and yellow core discarded
2 tomatoes, peeled and cut in half
salt and pepper
sugar
1 large canned truffle, drained and cut into julienne strips (optional)
2 tablespoons Madeira
½ cup heavy cream
1 teaspoon tarragon

Method
With a sharp knife cut the fish off the bone into 4 long portions and remove the bone.

To make fish stock: simmer the bone with the water, onion and peppercorns for 15 minutes, then strain.

To make sauce and garnish: melt 1 tablespoon butter in a small pan, add carrot and fish stock, cover and cook slowly for 5 minutes or until carrot is tender. Melt remaining butter, brush it over the tomatoes, sprinkle them with salt, pepper and a little sugar and broil them 4–5 inches from heat for 6–8 minutes, turning once, or bake them in a moderate oven (350°F) until tender.

Wash and dry fish pieces and roll them in seasoned flour. In a skillet heat oil, add 2 tablespoons butter and, when foaming, put in fish pieces and fry 5–6 minutes or until they flake easily and are golden brown on all sides. Lift carefully from pan, drain and arrange on a platter and keep warm.

If using truffle, add it to the carrot, pour over Madeira and bring to a boil. Add cream and season to taste. Place a spoonful of carrot and truffle julienne on each piece of fish and set half a tomato on top. Sprinkle with chopped tarragon and spoon remaining sauce around the platter.

Stuffed Trout Nantua

4 trout (¾–1 lb each)
1 quart quantity court bouillon (see box)

For shrimp mousse
½ lb cooked, peeled shrimps
thick béchamel sauce, made with 1½ tablespoons butter, 1½ tablespoons flour, ¾ cup milk (infused with slice of onion, 6 peppercorns, blade of mace and bay leaf)
¼ cup butter, softened
2 tablespoons heavy cream
salt and pepper
1½ cups mayonnaise (see page 86)
¼ teaspoon paprika
dash of Tabasco or 1 teaspoon tomato paste (or to taste)

For garnish
1 cucumber, peeled and diced or sliced
bunch of watercress, or ¼ lb cooked, peeled shrimps

Method
To prepare garnish: sprinkle the cucumber with salt and let stand 30 minutes to draw out the juices (dégorger). Rinse well and drain on paper towels.

Set the trout in a baking dish, pour over the court bouillon, cover with buttered foil and poach in a moderate oven (350°F) for 15–20 minutes or until the fish flakes easily when tested with a fork. Cool to tepid in the court bouillon, then drain and remove the skin and backbones.

To make the shrimp mousse: pass the shrimps twice through the fine blade of a grinder and beat into the béchamel sauce or work the ground shrimps with the sauce in a blender. Beat in the softened butter and cream and taste for seasoning.

Stuff each trout with shrimp mousse, reshape them and arrange diagonally on a platter. Season the mayonnaise with paprika and Tabasco or tomato paste to taste and thin it with hot water so it coats the back of a spoon.

Spoon a little mayonnaise over each trout and arrange the cucumber down one side of the platter, with the shrimps or watercress down the other side. Serve the rest of the mayonnaise separately.

Court Bouillon
For 1 quart quantity: in a pan combine 1 quart water, 1 sliced carrot, 1 sliced onion stuck with 1 clove, bouquet garni, 4 peppercorns, little salt and 1 cup white wine (or ¾ cup more water and ¼ cup white wine vinegar or lemon juice).

Cover, bring to a boil and simmer 30 minutes. Strain and use.

For 3 quart quantity, add 2 quarts water and double the remaining ingredients.

Seafood Vinaigrette

1 quart fresh mussels, cleaned, cooked and shelled (see Volume 10) or 1 can (9 oz) mussels, drained
1 cup (½ lb) crab meat
1½ cups (½ lb) cooked, peeled shrimps
2–3 medium beets, peeled, cooked and diced
4 small new potatoes, boiled, peeled and diced
1 cup fresh peas, cooked and drained, or 1 package frozen peas, cooked according to package directions
1 Delicious or other dessert apple
4–5 tablespoons olive oil
2 tablespoons white wine vinegar
1 clove of garlic, crushed
salt
black pepper, freshly ground
pinch of sugar (or to taste)
1½ cups mayonnaise (see page 86)

For garnish
bunch of watercress
3 hard-cooked eggs, quartered

Method
Put the mussels, crab meat and shrimps in a bowl with the diced beets, potatoes and peas. Wipe the apple, quarter, core, dice it and add to the fish mixture.

Mix the oil, vinegar, garlic, salt, pepper and a little sugar together, pour over the fish mixture and toss with 2 forks, adding more seasoning to taste. Cover and let stand to blend the flavors for 20 minutes, then add enough mayonnaise to bind the mixture lightly.

Pile the mixture on one half of a platter, garnish with the watercress and arrange hard-cooked eggs on the other side. Serve the rest of the mayonnaise separately.

Seafood vinaigrette is a colorful and appetizing salad

Strawberry mille feuilles is covered with the fruit and coated with red currant jelly glaze (recipe is on page 90)

A COLORFUL MENU

Crab Salad Printanier

Escalopes of Veal Valentino
Boiled New Potatoes

Strawberry Mille Feuilles

~~

White wine (for crab) — Puligny-Montrachet
(Côte de Beaune) or Pinot Chardonnay (California)

Red wine (for veal) — St. Emilion (Bordeaux)
or Cabernet Sauvignon (California)

An appetizer of artichoke bottoms filled with crab and topped with orange-flavored mayonnaise begins a colorful menu. The entrée is veal garnished with asparagus and for dessert there is a melting strawberry mille feuilles.

So opulent a first course suggests a particularly fine dry yet full-bodied white wine. The vineyards of Puligny-Montrachet, in Burgundy's Côte de Beaune district, produce some of the finest white wines. The best American counterpart of these wines is the Pinot Chardonnay from California's Napa Valley. The entrée will be well-matched by a red wine — at least five years old — from Bordeaux's St. Emilion district or a Cabernet Sauvignon from California.

TIMETABLE

Day before

Make puff pastry dough, wrap in plastic bag and chill. Brown and chop almonds for mille feuilles decoration. Make red currant jelly glaze.
Make mayonnaise and vinaigrette dressing for crab salad; prepare and cook artichoke bottoms, if necessary, and keep covered in refrigerator.

Morning

Roll out pastry dough and bake; cut in strips and keep covered with plastic wrap; crush trimmings and mix with almonds.
Hull strawberries, slice one-third and keep whole and sliced strawberries in refrigerator.
Prepare orange shreds and grate orange rind for crab salad; keep covered with plastic wrap. Wash lettuce leaves and store in plastic bag in refrigerator.
Cook asparagus. Cook veal escalopes and leave with mushrooms and asparagus in pan in refrigerator. Cut zucchini in strips, blanch, drain and put in pan with butter ready for cooking. Peel new potatoes and keep in cold water; chop parsley.

Assemble ingredients for final cooking from 7:00 for dinner around 8 p.m.

Order of Work

7:00
Make Chantilly cream, fill and complete mille feuilles; keep in refrigerator.

7:15
Complete salad printanier, cover with plastic wrap and keep in refrigerator.
Boil new potatoes.

7:45
Reheat veal on top of stove over low heat until very hot; cook zucchini in butter.
Spoon zucchini on heat-proof platter, arrange veal on top, spoon over sauce, sprinkle with crumbs and cheese and brown under broiler.

8:00
Serve appetizer.
Toss new potatoes in butter and add parsley just before serving.

You will find that **cooking times** given in the individual recipes for these dishes have sometimes been adapted in the timetable to help you when cooking and serving this menu as a party meal.

Appetizer

Crab Salad Printanier

¾ lb crab meat
4 fresh artichokes or 4 canned artichoke bottoms
¼ cup ripe olives, pitted and halved
2 tablespoons vinaigrette dressing (see page 44)
1 orange
1 cup mayonnaise
4 large lettuce leaves

Method

To prepare fresh artichoke bottoms, cut off the stalks and pull away the lower leaves. Cut tops off the remaining leaves, leaving about 1 inch at base. Cook the artichokes in boiling salted water for 20–25 minutes or until tender, drain and cool slightly. Pull away the remaining leaves and scoop out the hairy chokes with a teaspoon. Drain canned artichokes. Spoon the vinaigrette dressing over artichoke bottoms, cover and let stand to marinate until cold.

With a vegetable peeler, remove a strip of rind from the orange and cut it in needle-like shreds. Blanch the orange shreds in boiling water for 5 minutes and drain. Finely grate the remaining orange rind to give 2 teaspoons and squeeze juice from orange.

Flavor the mayonnaise to taste with orange juice and the finely grated rind and thin it, if necessary, until it coats the back of a spoon.

Arrange the lettuce leaves on 4 individual salad plates, place an artichoke heart on top and pile on the crab meat. Spoon over the mayonnaise and garnish with shredded orange rind and halved olives.

Mayonnaise

For 1 cup: in a bowl beat 2 egg yolks with ¼ teaspoon salt and pinch each of pepper and dry mustard with a small whisk or wooden spoon until thick. Measure ¾ cup oil. Add 2 tablespoons oil drop by drop, beating constantly; the mixture will then be very thick. Stir in 1 teaspoon wine vinegar. Remaining oil can be added more quickly (1 tablespoon at a time, beaten thoroughly between each addition until smooth, or in a thin steady stream if using a blender). When all oil has been added, add 1½ tablespoons more wine vinegar with more seasoning to taste. To thin and lighten mayonnaise, add a little hot water.

Watchpoint: mayonnaise curdles very easily, so add the oil drop by drop at first, then very slowly until mayonnaise is thick, when you can add the oil in a slow steady stream. If mayonnaise curdles, start with a fresh yolk in another bowl and work well with seasonings. Then add curdled mixture drop by drop. Be sure all ingredients are at room temperature before starting. Increase quantities, depending on your needs.

Crab salad printanier is garnished with shredded orange rind and halved ripe olives

Escalopes of veal Valentino are garnished with asparagus and served with boiled small new potatoes tossed in butter and chopped parsley

Ingredients for the escalopes of veal Valentino include mushrooms and asparagus

Entrée

Escalopes of Veal Valentino

4–8 veal escalopes (about 1½ lb)
¼ cup clarified butter
1 tablespoon flour
1 cup veal or chicken stock
1 cup light cream
salt
black pepper, freshly ground
1 cup (¼ lb) mushrooms, sliced
squeeze of lemon juice
1 lb fresh asparagus, cooked
3–4 zucchini, peeled, seeds
    removed and cut in 2 inch
    strips
2 tablespoons butter
2 tablespoons grated
    Parmesan cheese

Method
If necessary, place the escalopes between 2 sheets of wax paper and pound them with a mallet or rolling pin until thin.

Heat the clarified butter in a large sauté or frying pan, add the escalopes and cook for 3–4 minutes on each side or until browned. Remove from the pan and keep warm. Stir the flour into the pan and cook it, stirring constantly, until lightly browned. Stir in the stock and cream, season and bring to a boil. Add the sliced mushrooms with a squeeze of lemon juice and replace the veal escalopes in the pan. Simmer over low heat for 5–6 minutes until the veal is tender. Add the cooked asparagus and cook 1–2 minutes longer or until very hot.

Blanch the zucchini in boiling salted water for 1 minute, drain and cook quickly in the butter in a covered pan for 1–2 minutes or until tender. Season with salt and pepper.

Spoon zucchini into an ovenproof serving dish, lay the veal escalopes, overlapping, on top, taste for seasoning and spoon over the sauce. Arrange the asparagus on top, sprinkle with Parmesan cheese and broil until browned. Serve with boiled small new potatoes tossed in butter and parsley.

To Cook Fresh Asparagus

Trim the white part from the asparagus stalks so they are the same length. Rinse them in cold water and with a vegetable peeler remove the tough skin from the lower ends of the stems. Tie asparagus stalks in several bundles and stand these, stems down, in 1–2 inches boiling salted water in an asparagus cooker or tall pan. Cover and simmer 8–10 minutes or until the green tips are just tender. Lift bundles carefully from pan, drain on paper towels and remove strings.

Accompaniment to entrée

Boiled New Potatoes

If potatoes are very small, scrub them or scrape them with a pot scrubber to remove the skin. If larger, peel with a vegetable peeler. Put them in boiling salted water and boil, uncovered, for 15–20 minutes or until just tender when pierced with a knife; they should still be firm and waxy in consistency. Drain them, return to the pan and toss for 1 minute over low heat with butter and chopped parsley.

Dessert

Strawberry Mille Feuilles

1 quart strawberries, hulled
1½ cup quantity puff pastry
¼ cup browned, slivered
    almonds, finely chopped
Chantilly cream (made with
    1 cup heavy cream, stiffly
    whipped and sweetened
    with 1 tablespoon sugar,
    ½ teaspoon vanilla)
½ cup red currant jelly glaze

Method

Set the oven at hot (425°F).

Roll out the pastry dough as thinly as possible to a large rectangle. Lay this on a dampened baking sheet, letting the dough come sligthly over the edge. Prick dough well all over with a fork and chill 10 minutes. Bake in heated oven for 10–15 minutes or until browned. Loosen the pastry with a spatula and turn it over. Bake 5 minutes longer, then transfer to a wire rack to cool. When cold, trim the edges and cut pastry into 3 strips, each about 3 inches wide; crush the trimmings lightly and mix them with the almonds.

Slice about one-third of the strawberries, mix with half the Chantilly cream and spread over 1 strip of pastry. Place a second strip of pastry on top, spread with the remaining Chantilly cream and cover with the last strip of pastry. Brush the top with red currant jelly glaze.

Cut remaining strawberries in half and arrange them neatly on top of the pastry. Brush again with red currant jelly glaze and cover the sides of the bottom layer

of the mille feuilles with the pastry trimmings mixture.

Cut the mille feuilles into slices to serve.

For strawberry mille feuilles, place second pastry strip on the strawberry mixture

Cover the sides of the bottom layer with crushed pastry trimmings and almond mixture

Puff Pastry

2 cups flour
1 cup butter
pinch of salt
1 teaspoon lemon juice
½–¾ cup ice water

You will need only 1½ cup quantity of puff pastry for the mille feuilles. Use the trimmings to make small pastries like palmiers, jalousie or sacristans (see Volume 8).

Method

Reserve 1 tablespoon of butter and place the rest, lightly floured, between 2 pieces of wax paper. Pound with a rolling pin, remove the top piece of wax paper, fold the butter in half, replace the wax paper and pound again. Continue in this way until the butter is pliable but not sticky. Shape into a 5 inch square, dust lightly with flour and chill until firm but not hard.

Sift flour and salt into a bowl or onto a marble slab and rub in the reserved 1 tablespoon butter. Add the lemon juice to ½ cup of the water. Make a well in the center of the flour and pour in the water and lemon juice. Mix with a spatula or round-bladed knife in the bowl or use your fingers on a marble slab. When a dough begins to form, add most of the remaining water. Mix to a firm, pliable dough, adding the remaining water if necessary.

Lightly dust a marble slab or work surface with flour and knead the dough for 1–2 minutes. Roll out to a 12-inch square.

Place the butter in the center of the dough and fold it over the butter, wrapping the sides and ends over like a parcel. Wrap in plastic wrap or a plastic bag and chill 15 minutes.

Sprinkle the work surface lightly with flour, put down the dough with the joins facing up, and bring the rolling pin firmly down on the dough 3–4 times to flatten it slightly.

Roll out to a rectangle about 5–6 inches wide and almost 3 times as long. Fold it into three, one end over the other, as accurately as possible; if necessary pull the corners to keep them in a rectangle. Seal edges with the rolling pin and turn the dough half around to bring the open edges towards you. Roll out again and fold in three. Keep a note of the 'turns' made by marking the dough lightly with the appropriate number of fingerprints. Wrap and chill 15 minutes.

Repeat this process, giving the dough 6 turns altogether with a 15 minute rest after every 2 turns. Wrap and refrigerate until needed.

CHAUDFROIDS AND GALANTINES

Few displays can equal the splendor of a lavish buffet table set with a colorful array of contrasting platters. Chaudfroids and galantines are among the dishes that have been created especially for such occasions.

Like all cold dishes, chaudfroids and galantines must be highly seasoned because chilling diminishes their flavor. They take time to prepare, but are ideal for a party, as the protective coating of aspic prevents the food from drying out, so the dish can be prepared up to 12 hours in advance.

CHAUDFROIDS

Chaudfroid means literally 'hot-cold' and a chaudfroid is a cold dish of cooked fish, poultry or game that is first coated with a sauce called a chaudfroid, then finished with a shiny layer of aspic.

The name chaudfroid comes from the sauce that is simmered over heat, then cooled before using to coat the cooked food.

To make chaudfroid sauce, a little aspic and gelatin are added to a basic white or brown sauce to ensure the sauce sets firmly when cold. The aspic is made with fish, chicken or veal stock, depending on the food to be coated.

There are 3 basic sauces:

1 White chaudfroid sauce is based on a creamy béchamel or well-flavored velouté sauce to which aspic and gelatin are added. Use for coating eggs, fish, veal or chicken.

2 Aurore chaudfroid sauce is a white béchamel-based chaudfroid sauce that has been flavored and colored with a tomato mixture. Use for coating fish, eggs and chicken.

3 Brown chaudfroid sauce is based on an Espagnole or brown sauce, with aspic and gelatin added, plus a little port or sherry for flavor. Use with duck, goose and game.

Points to remember

1 The consistency of a chaudfroid sauce is most important – if it is too thick, the surface will be lumpy, if it is too thin, the sauce slides off the food. Before the aspic is added, the basic sauce should thinly coat the back of a spoon.

2 Ideally the sauce should be tammied after it is made, to give additional gloss (see box).

3 Like aspic, chaudfroid sauce is spooned over food when the sauce is just on the point of setting. It will set quickly, though not as suddenly as aspic, and at this stage it should coat the back of a spoon fairly thickly.

4 Set the food to be coated on a wire rack over a tray to catch drips during the coating process; then chill it well. Chill the chaudfroid sauce, stirring, over a bowl of ice water. As soon as it starts to set, spoon the sauce quickly and evenly over the cold food.

5 Often 2 coats of sauce are necessary. To do this, chill the food again until the first coating of sauce is firmly set. Melt the remaining sauce, chill it over ice water and repeat the coating.

6 Add decoration and 1–2 coatings of aspic on top of the chaudfroid sauce as described in the feature on gelatins in Volume 8.

White Chaudfroid Sauce 1

2 tablespoons butter
2 tablespoons flour
2 cups milk (infused with slice of onion, 6 peppercorns, blade of mace and bay leaf)
3 tablespoons heavy cream
salt and pepper
1 envelope gelatin
$\frac{1}{2}$ cup cool but still liquid aspic, made with fish, chicken or veal stock

Makes $2\frac{1}{2}$ cups béchamel-based chaudfroid sauce or enough to coat a large chicken chaudfroid. Use any leftover sauce as hot béchamel sauce or add it to soup.

Method
In a saucepan melt the butter and, when foaming, take from the heat and stir in the flour. Strain in the infused milk and bring to a boil, stirring constantly. Add the cream, simmer 1–2 minutes, taste for seasoning, take from the heat and cover tightly with plastic wrap to prevent a skin from forming. Let the sauce cool.

Sprinkle the gelatin over the cool but still liquid aspic, let stand 5 minutes until spongy and dissolve over a pan of hot water. Stir the aspic into the sauce and work it through a tammy strainer or wring through cheesecloth. Taste the sauce again for seasoning, cool it and use when on the point of setting.

The term **chaudfroid** is thought to date from mid-18th century, when the Maréchal de Luxembourg, who was giving a banquet, was suddenly called away. On returning late he tasted only one dish – a fricassée of chicken grown cold in its own sauce. It was so delicious he demanded the dish be repeated and began a fashion for chaudfroid.

White Chaudfroid Sauce 2

For a velouté-based chaudfroid sauce, substitute $1\frac{1}{2}$ cups well-flavored fish, chicken or veal stock for the infused milk in white chaudfroid sauce 1 and $\frac{3}{4}$ cup instead of 3 tablespoons heavy cream.

Aurore Chaudfroid Sauce
(Tomato Chaudfroid Sauce)

white chaudfroid sauce 1
    (see left), made with
    1½ tablespoons butter,
    1½ tablespoons flour,
    1½ cups infused milk,
    3 tablespoons heavy cream,
    salt and pepper
½ cup cool but still liquid aspic,
    made with fish, chicken or
    veal stock
1 envelope gelatin

For tomato mixture
2 medium ripe tomatoes,
    quartered and seeded, or
    1 cup (8 oz) canned
    tomatoes
bouquet garni
1 clove of garlic, peeled
1 teaspoon tomato paste
    (optional)

Makes about 2½ cups.

Method

To make tomato mixture: in a pan combine tomatoes, bouquet garni and garlic and simmer gently, stirring often, until soft and thick. Season to taste and add tomato paste if tomatoes were not very ripe. Work mixture through a fine sieve — it should make ½ cup purée.

Make the chaudfroid sauce as for chaudfroid sauce 1, adding the tomato purée before stirring in the aspic and gelatin.

Brown Chaudfroid Sauce

2 cups well-reduced Espagnole
    sauce
¼ cup sherry
1 teaspoon tomato paste
    (optional)
¼ cup cool but still liquid aspic,
    made with veal, beef or
    game stock
1 envelope gelatin

Makes 2½ cups or enough sauce to coat a large duck or pheasant chaudfroid.

Method

Add the sherry to Espagnole sauce and simmer 2–3 minutes. Cover tightly with plastic wrap and let cool.
Watchpoint: the color and flavor of the brown sauce are most important — if necessary, add 1 teaspoon tomato paste with the sherry to improve its appearance and taste.

Sprinkle the gelatin over the cool but still liquid aspic, let stand 5 minutes until spongy and dissolve over a pan of hot water. Stir into Espagnole sauce, then work through a tammy strainer or wring through cheesecloth. Taste the sauce for seasoning, cool it and use when on the point of setting.

To Tammy Sauce

This process binds fat and flour together and gives the sauce a particularly smooth, glossy finish.

Either work the sauce with a whisk through a very fine, double-mesh wire sieve called a tammy strainer or squeeze it through a rough-textured cloth or a double layer of cheesecloth.

If no tammy strainer is available, use the finest regular sieve. Or, if using cheesecloth, soak it in boiling water, wring out and lay over a bowl. Pour in the sauce, fold the sides of the cloth over the sauce to enclose it completely and wring out until all sauce has been forced through. (Two pairs of hands make this operation easier.)

Poultry Chaudfroid

There are 2 ways of making this:
1 The bird is poached, cut in pieces when cold; each piece is coated with white chaudfroid sauce, decorated, and glazed with aspic (see recipe on page 97).
2 A large chicken, preferably a capon (a neutered cock bird) or a poularde (a hen bird), or a turkey is poached, skinned and the suprêmes (breast meat and bones) are carefully cut away. The cavity is filled with a mousse of ham, chicken or foie gras, then the suprêmes are sliced and replaced on the mousse. Finally, the whole bird is coated and decorated as in the method above. This elaborate dish is usually served for a special occasion. (See recipe for chicken or turkey Rose Marie on page 97).

Chicken chaudfroid, decorated with sliced mushrooms and pieces of pimiento and truffle, is arranged on chopped aspic

Chicken Chaudfroid

$3\frac{1}{2}$–4 lb roasting chicken
1 onion
1 carrot
1 stalk of celery
bouquet garni
salt and pepper
2 cups aspic
$1\frac{1}{2}$ cups white chaudfroid
    sauce 1 (see page 94)

To decorate
fresh chervil or tarragon,
    mushrooms, pimiento or
    truffle
2 cups aspic, set and chopped
bunch of watercress
    (for garnish)

Method
In a covered kettle poach the chicken with vegetables, bouquet garni, salt and pepper and water just to cover thigh bone. Cook 45–55 minutes or until bird is tender and no pink juice runs out when thigh is pierced with a skewer; let cool in cooking liquid. Then take out and strain liquid and use to make 4 cups aspic.
Watchpoint: do not add too much water to the chicken as the cooking liquid must be very concentrated to give flavor to aspic in the chaudfroid sauce. Keep pan tightly covered during cooking so the liquid does not evaporate too much.
Make the chaudfroid sauce.
Cut the chicken into neat pieces, discarding skin and backbone, and trim as much bone as possible from each piece. Lay pieces on a wire rack over a tray and chill thoroughly.
Cool the chaudfroid sauce over a pan of ice water, stirring until on the point of setting, then quickly spoon over the cold chicken pieces. Chill, then coat again with sauce if

they are not neatly covered.
Decorate the chicken pieces with blanched sprigs of chervil or tarragon, sliced, cooked mushrooms, or pieces of sliced pimiento or truffle, dipping each piece of decoration in aspic so it adheres to the chicken. Chill well, then coat with aspic on the point of setting. Pour remaining aspic into a dampened tray, chill until set, then chop it. Chill again for at least 1 hour so the aspic and sauce are firmly set. Spread roughly chopped aspic on a chilled platter and arrange chicken pieces on top. Garnish the platter with watercress before serving.

Chicken or Turkey Rose Marie

5–6 lb chicken or turkey
1 onion, sliced
1 carrot, sliced
1 stalk of celery, sliced
bouquet garni
salt and pepper
$2\frac{1}{2}$ cups aurore chaudfroid
    sauce (see page 95)
4 cups aspic

For mousse
1 lb lean cooked ham or
    cooked veal
béchamel sauce, made with
    $1\frac{1}{2}$ tablespoons butter,
    $1\frac{1}{2}$ tablespoons flour,
    $1\frac{1}{2}$ cups milk (infused with
    slice of onion, 6 peppercorns,
    blade of mace and bay leaf)
$\frac{1}{2}$ cup unsalted butter
$\frac{3}{4}$ cup heavy cream, whipped
    until it holds a soft shape

For garnish
$1\frac{1}{2}$–2 lb fresh asparagus,
    trimmed, cooked and
    drained, or 2 packages frozen
    asparagus, cooked according
    to package directions and
    drained

This recipe gives the second method of making chicken chaudfroid, in which the bird is stuffed with a mousse mixture and reshaped. Serves 6–8 people.

Method
In a covered kettle poach the bird with vegetables, bouquet garni, salt and pepper and water just to cover the thigh bone. Cook $1\frac{1}{4}$–$1\frac{1}{2}$ hours or until the bird is just tender and no pink juice runs out when the thigh is pierced with a skewer.
Watchpoint: it is important that the bird is not overcooked. Keep pan tightly covered during cooking so the liquid does not evaporate too much.
Let the bird cool in the liquid, then take out and strain the liquid and use to make 4 cups aspic.
Make the aurore chaudfroid sauce, cover tightly with plastic wrap and let cool.
To make the mousse: make the béchamel sauce, cover with plastic wrap and chill it. Work the ham or veal twice through the fine blade of the grinder and pound it in a mortar and pestle with the béchamel sauce. Or, instead of pounding, work the ground meat with the béchamel sauce for a few moments in a blender, a little at a time. Cream the butter, beat it into the meat mixture, then stir in $\frac{1}{2}$ cup cool but still liquid aspic and fold in the cream. Taste mousse for seasoning.
Remove the skin from the bird and discard it. With a sharp knife cut away the suprêmes. Cut away breast bone and ribs of the bird and discard them. Cut suprêmes in thin slices.
Fill the body cavity with mousse mixture, mounding it up well, and replace the suprêmes on the mousse

leaving an open space down the center. Chill the bird thoroughly, then fill the space with a few spoonsful of aspic on the point of setting, smoothing the top. Set the bird on a wire rack and chill again.
Chill the aurore chaudfroid sauce over ice water until it is just on point of setting, then coat bird, chill it until set, then coat again with the remaining sauce.
Split several stalks of asparagus lengthwise and arrange them, overlapping, down the breast in the open space. Coat the bird all over with aspic that is on the point of setting and chill. Pour some of the remaining aspic into a dampened shallow tray and chill until set.
When set, turn the aspic out onto a damp sheet of wax or silicone paper and cut out 2–3 inch rounds, diamonds or crescents. Arrange these as a border around the edge of a chilled silver or stainless steel platter. Chop the remaining aspic and spread it in the bottom of platter. Set the bird on the chopped aspic and arrange remaining asparagus in bunches on the platter; baste the asparagus with a little cool but still liquid aspic. Chill the platter well before serving.

Cut the suprêmes down from top of the breastbone with a sharp knife, taking care to keep the knife close to the rib cage. Detach the white meat in one piece, with the wing bone

GALANTINES

A galantine is a dish made with a boned chicken, turkey, duck or game bird, or with a boned breast of veal that is spread with stuffing, rolled, then sewn or tied and poached in stock.

The galantine is left to cool. Then it is either sliced and coated with sherry-flavored aspic or it may be left whole, coated with a chaudfroid sauce, then decorated and coated with aspic. When served whole, a galantine makes a splendid buffet centerpiece.

Galantine de Volaille
(Chicken Galantine)

4–4½ lb roasting chicken, with the giblets
1 calf's foot, scrubbed, split lengthwise and blanched (optional)
2 lb veal bones
1 onion, quartered
1 carrot, quartered
6 peppercorns
salt
4 cups aspic (made with stock from cooking chicken)
bunch of watercress (for garnish)

For stuffing
2 boned chicken breasts
2 tablespoons brandy
black pepper, freshly ground
½ lb piece bacon
¼ teaspoon ground allspice
¼ teaspoon ground nutmeg
thick slice (about ½ lb) cooked tongue
thick slice (about ½ lb) cooked lean ham
small can truffles, diced and liquid reserved

Trussing needle and string

Method

Bone the chicken and set it aside. For stock: break up the bones and neck and put in a large kettle with the gizzard, calf's foot, if used, veal bones, onion, carrot, peppercorns, a little salt and water to cover. Cover the pan and simmer 1–1½ hours; strain the stock.

To make stuffing: cut the chicken breasts in strips, discarding the skin, pour over the brandy, sprinkle with pepper and leave to marinate ½–1 hour. Blanch the bacon in boiling water for 10 minutes, drain and cut it in pieces.

Lay the boned chicken on a board, skin side down, and carefully cut the meat from the skin, discarding any sinews and leaving the skin in one piece. Work the chicken meat with the bacon through the fine blade of a grinder. Add any marinade from the chicken strips (do not grind strips), the spices and plenty of seasoning and mix well. Cut the ham and tongue into strips.

Lay a cloth or piece of cheesecloth on a board and spread the chicken skin on top, inside up. Spread a fifth of the stuffing in the middle of the skin in a 9 X 3 inch rectangle and lay half the strips of chicken on top. Add a layer of stuffing, then a layer of all the ham strips, then another layer of stuffing. Scatter over the diced truffles, cover with the tongue strips, add another layer of stuffing, top with the remaining chicken strips and the remaining stuffing.

Carefully wrap the chicken skin around the stuffing to form a cylinder. Sew the cylinder along the seam with a trussing needle and string, then roll it tightly in the cloth or cheesecloth; tie the ends and fasten the overlap with a safety pin. Put the chicken stock in a kettle, lower in the galantine, cover and simmer gently 1½ hours or until a skewer inserted in the center of the galantine for 1 minute is very hot to the touch when withdrawn.

Let the galantine cool to lukewarm in the stock, then rewrap the cloth tightly around it and fasten again. Set the galantine between two plates or boards with a 4 lb weight on top and chill overnight in the refrigerator. Boil the stock to reduce it to 4 cups if necessary and use it to make aspic.

Cut the galantine in three-eighth inch slices and arrange them, overlapping, on a large silver or stainless steel platter. Chill thoroughly, then coat with aspic that is on the point of setting. Chill, and add another coating of aspic. Chill thoroughly. Pour the remaining aspic into a shallow tray, chill until set, then turn out and chop it. Decorate the platter with chopped aspic and a bunch of watercress.

Galantine of Pheasant

1 large plump pheasant
salt
black pepper, freshly ground
1 onion, sliced
1 carrot, sliced
1 stalk of celery, sliced
bouquet garni
2 tablespoons sherry
½ envelope gelatin (optional)

For stuffing
½ lb ground veal or pork
¼ lb cooked lean ham, ground
½ cup fresh white breadcrumbs
2 shallots or 1 onion, finely chopped
1½ tablespoons butter
1 teaspoon sage or marjoram
1 tablespoon chopped parsley
1–2 tablespoons sherry
pinch of ground mace or nutmeg
1 small egg, beaten to mix

Trussing needle and string

This galantine improves in flavor if it is made 1–2 days ahead. Serves 6–8 people.

Method
Bone the pheasant as for a chicken, spread the bird out on a board, skin side down, and season the cut surfaces well.

Break up the carcass bones and put them in a pan with the vegetables, bouquet garni, seasoning and water to cover. Cover pan, simmer 1½–2 hours and strain the stock.

To make the stuffing: mix the ground veal or pork, ham and breadcrumbs together. Cook the shallots or onion in the butter until soft but not brown and stir into the meat mixture with the herbs and sherry. Add the spice with plenty of seasoning and add enough egg to bind the mixture without making it wet. Spread the stuffing evenly over the pheasant and roll it up to a neat cylinder, starting at one side and tucking in the ends. Sew it with a trussing needle and fine string.

Roll the galantine tightly in a cloth or piece of cheesecloth, tie the ends and fasten the overlap with a safety pin.

Put the pheasant stock in a kettle, lower in the galantine, cover and simmer gently for about $1\frac{1}{2}$ hours or until a skewer inserted in the center of the galantine for 1 minute is very hot to the touch when withdrawn.

Let the galantine cool to lukewarm in the stock, then rewrap the cloth tightly around it and fasten again. Set the galantine between 2 plates or boards with a 4 lb weight on top and chill overnight in the refrigerator. Boil the pheasant stock to reduce it to $1-1\frac{1}{2}$ cups, strain, add the sherry, taste for seasoning and chill — the stock should be firmly set; if it is not, sprinkle over $\frac{1}{2}$ envelope gelatin, let stand 5 minutes until spongy and dissolve over gentle heat.

To serve, untie the galantine and discard the string. Arrange the galantine on a platter, whole or cut in three-eighth inch slices.

Melt pheasant stock and stir over a bowl of ice water until on the point of setting. Spoon over the galantine to glaze it. Serve a salad separately such as celery, apple and walnut salad (see Volume 6) or orange, celery and chestnut salad (see page 100).

Galantine of Duck

4–5 lb duck, with the giblets
1 calf's foot, scrubbed, split lengthwise and blanched (optional)
2 lb veal bones
salt and pepper
2 veal kidneys
$\frac{1}{4}$ cup sherry
1 tablespoon oil
2 onions, sliced
2 carrots, sliced
bouquet garni
1 quart well-flavored chicken or veal stock
2$\frac{1}{2}$ cups brown or white chaudfroid sauce 1 (see pages 94–95)
bunch of watercress (for garnish)

For stuffing
$\frac{3}{4}$ lb ground veal
1 lb ground pork, including some fat
salt
black pepper, freshly ground
$\frac{1}{3}$ cup heavy cream
small can truffle pieces (optional)
$\frac{1}{4}$ cup pistachios

Trussing needle and string

This galantine can be made 1–2 days ahead. Serves 6–8 people.

Method
Bone the duck and set it aside. Break up the bones and neck and put them in a large kettle with the duck gizzard, calf's foot, if used, the veal bones, seasoning and water to cover. Cover the pan and simmer 1–1$\frac{1}{2}$ hours; strain the cooking liquid.

Lay the duck on a board, skin side down, and carefully detach the meat from the skin, leaving the skin in 1 piece. Cut the breast and leg meat into strips, discarding any sinews, and reserving any small pieces of meat. Cut the core from the veal kidneys and slice them. Combine with the duck meat and pour over the sherry. Cover and let marinate 2 hours.

Drain the truffles, reserving the liquid, thinly slice them and cut crescents, diamonds, etc., with a small knife and a large plain tube or sharp bottle top. Chop leftover pieces of truffle.

To make the stuffing: finely chop the reserved pieces of duck meat with the duck liver and mix them with the ground veal and pork and plenty of seasoning. Stir in the cream with the chopped truffles and liquid if used, and any marinade drained from the duck and veal kidneys. Blanch the pistachios in boiling water for $\frac{1}{2}$ minute, drain and add to the stuffing.

Lay a cloth or piece of cheesecloth on a board or table and spread the duck skin on top with the inside of the skin up. Then spread one-third of the stuffing in the middle of the duck skin in a 9 X 3 inch rectangle and lay half the strips of duck and veal kidneys lengthwise on top. Add another layer of stuffing, then arrange the remaining duck and veal kidneys on top and spread with the remaining stuffing. Carefully wrap the duck skin around the meat and stuffing to form a cylinder. Sew the cylinder along the seam with a trussing needle and string, then roll it tightly in the cloth or cheesecloth; tie the ends and fasten the overlap with a safety pin.

In a deep flameproof casserole heat the oil and cook the onions and carrots until brown. Lay the galantine on top, pour over the stock (it should cover the galantine), add the bouquet garni and simmer 1$\frac{1}{2}$ hours or until a skewer inserted in the center of the galantine for 1 minute is hot to the touch when withdrawn.

Let the galantine cool to lukewarm, then lift it out, unwrap the cloth, tighten it and tie it again. Set the galantine between 2 boards or plates, with a 4 lb weight on top and chill overnight. Strain the stock and use it to make aspic.

The next day, make the brown or white chaudfroid sauce, cover tightly and cool.

Set the galantine on a wire rack over a tray, stir the chaudfroid sauce over a bowl of ice water until on the point of setting and spoon it over the galantine. Chill the galantine and repeat the coating of sauce, if necessary.

Moisten the truffle decorations with a little aspic so they adhere to the galantine and arrange them on top. Chill well.

Set the galantine on a wire rack and coat it with aspic. Chill, repeat the coating of aspic, if necessary. Pour the remaining aspic into a tray, chill until set, then turn out and cut out crescents, diamonds, etc., for decoration.

Set the galantine on a platter, decorate the edge with aspic shapes and add a bunch of watercress.

Orange, Celery and Chestnut Salad

2 oranges
small bunch of celery, cut in julienne strips
$\frac{1}{2}$ lb chestnuts, peeled
1 cup stock
$\frac{1}{2}$ cup vinaigrette dressing (see page 44)
$\frac{1}{2}$ teaspoon sugar (or to taste)

This salad is an ideal accompaniment to game dishes.

Method
Soak the celery in ice water for 30 minutes to make it crisp, then drain thoroughly. Simmer the chestnuts in stock for 20–30 minutes or until tender and drain them. Cut the peel and pith from the oranges with a serrated-edge knife and slice them. Mix the oranges, celery and chestnuts, toss with vinaigrette dressing and sugar to taste and serve.

Galantine of duck is coated with chaudfroid sauce and decorated with pieces of truffle

Buffet for a golden wedding anniversary includes a croquembouche tower, cold stuffed duck with spiced apricots, gold cake, apricot ice cream (at back), potage crème d'or and a caramel basket filled with petits fours

GOLDEN WEDDING ANNIVERSARY IDEAS

Celebrate a golden wedding anniversary or any special day with a buffet for 16 that develops the golden theme in dishes like cold stuffed duck with spiced apricots and a caramel basket filled with petits fours. Or plan a seated buffet for 12 with golden stuffed eggs, chicken balls in a rich mushroom sauce and a tempting apricot mold served with chocolate and praline candies.

BUFFET FOR 16

Potage Crème d'Or
or
Mousseline of Sole

Cold Stuffed Duck
Spiced Apricots

Golden Fruit Gelatin
Gold Cake

Caramel Basket
with Petits Fours

Croquembouche

Apricot Ice Cream

Refer to following Volumes for these dishes: Volume 8 for **lemon gelatin** (for golden fruit gelatin); Volume 11 for **fruit ice cream** and Volume 5 for **tuiles** (for apricot ice cream).

TIMETABLE

Several days before
Make gold cake and store in an airtight container; make the fondant icing and keep sealed.
Make petits fours and store in an airtight container.
Make apricot ice cream and store in freezer.
Make spiced apricots and seal in jars.

Day before
Make potage crème d'or and chill.
Make aspic for sole and duck. Make mousseline of sole and chill; do not coat with aspic.
Roast duck and cool; fill with stuffing, cover and keep in refrigerator.
Make dressing for salad.
Make fruit gelatin, cover tightly and chill.
Bake round of French flan pastry for croquembouche; store in airtight container.
Decorate gold cake and keep covered.

Morning
Coat sole with aspic and store in refrigerator.
Coat duck with aspic, decorate, keep in refrigerator.
Make cream puffs and finish croquembouche.
Make caramel basket and keep in cool dry place.
Prepare vegetables for salad and keep in plastic bags in refrigerator.

Just before serving
Scoop out ice cream into chilled bowl.
Fill caramel basket with petits fours or ice cream.
Spoon the soup into cups and add garnish.
Toss salad with dressing.
Unmold fruit gelatin.

Potage Crème d'Or

10 medium-sized young carrots, sliced
$\frac{1}{2}$ tablespoon sugar
salt and pepper
$\frac{1}{3}$ cup butter
2 medium onions, finely chopped
$2\frac{1}{2}$ quarts chicken stock
juice of 2 oranges
2 cups heavy cream
chopped chives (for garnish)

This recipe was originally given in Volume 15. The quantity given here serves 16 people.

Method
In a covered pan simmer the carrots with the sugar, salt and pepper, and water to cover for 15 minutes or until the carrots are tender. Drain them.
Watchpoint: if the carrots are not very young, discard the hard yellow core before cooking.

In a pan melt the butter, add the onion and cook over a low heat until soft but not brown. Add the carrots and cook them gently until the butter is absorbed.

Work the mixture through a sieve or food mill, or purée in a blender with a little of the stock. Mix the carrot purée with the remaining stock, orange juice, seasoning and cream and stir gently until well mixed. Taste for seasoning and chill thoroughly. Before serving, add the chives.

Mousseline of Sole

3–4 medium sole fillets, cut in half lengthwise
1 lb cooked, peeled shrimps

For mousseline
$1\frac{1}{2}$ lb haddock fillet
4 egg whites, beaten until broken up
$1\frac{1}{2}$ cups heavy cream
salt and pepper

To finish
2 cups cool but still liquid aspic
1 cup mayonnaise (see page 86)
1–2 tablespoons hot water
bunch of watercress (for garnish)

Ring mold (1 quart capacity)

Serves 8 people.

Method
Place the sole fillets between 2 sheets of wax paper and pound lightly with a mallet to flatten them. Generously butter the ring mold.

Arrange the fillets in the mold with the skinned sides up and tail ends to the center, making sure the fillets overlap slightly. The bottom and sides of the mold should be completely covered. Chill.

To make the mousseline: pass the haddock twice through the fine blade of a grinder. Pound the fish in a mortar and pestle and gradually work in the egg whites. Or instead of pounding, work ground fish and egg whites for a few seconds in a blender until very smooth. Gradually beat in the cream and add seasoning.

Spoon the mousseline into the fish-lined mold, smoothing it level with the top; reserve any mousseline left over. Fold the ends of the fillets over onto the mousseline and cover with a piece of buttered foil. Stand the mold in a water bath and poach in a moderate oven (350°F) for about 45 minutes or until the mousseline is firm to the touch.

Remove the mold from the oven and let cool to tepid. Turn out the mold onto a platter, preferably made of silver or stainless steel. With paper towels wipe away any liquid that drains from the mold; cover and chill it.

Shape the remaining mousseline with 2 soup spoons to form quenelles and poach them in gently simmering salted water for 6–7 minutes or until firm to the touch. Drain them well and let cool.

To finish the mold: spoon a layer of cool but still liquid aspic over the mold to coat it: Chill until set and repeat the coating once or twice. Put 1 tablespoon mayonnaise in the center of the mold, pile the shrimps and quenelles on top and coat them with the remaining mayonnaise (thinned to a coating consistency with 1–2 tablespoons hot water).

Garnish the platter with watercress.

Cold Stuffed Duck

2 ducks (5 lb each)
salt and pepper
about 1 cup chicken stock or
  stock made from giblets (not
  livers) of the ducks
2 tablespoons honey
4 cups aspic
bunch of watercress (for
  garnish)

For stuffing
livers of the ducks
1 tablespoon oil
1½ lb cooked ham, coarsely
  chopped
1 can (½ lb) liver pâté
1 tablespoon chopped parsley
1 tablespoon mixed herbs –
  thyme, oregano
⅓ cup sherry

Serves 8 people.

Method
Set oven at hot (400°F).

Season the duck cavities well and place the ducks on a rack in a roasting pan. Prick the skin to release fat and roast in heated oven. Baste the ducks frequently during cooking and turn them from one side to the other. After 30 minutes, drain off most of the fat and add about ½ cup of the stock to the pan. Roast 1–1¼ hours longer or until no pink juice runs out when the thighs are pierced with a skewer. About 30 minutes before the end of the cooking, set the ducks on their backs and put 1 tablespoon honey in the cavity of each. Complete the roasting.

Remove the ducks with the rack and let them cool. Discard the fat from the pan and deglaze the pan juices with the remaining stock; strain and chill.

To prepare the stuffing: sauté the duck livers in the oil until browned but still pink in the center, then work them through a grinder with the chopped ham. Work in the pâté, herbs and sherry, and season the stuffing well.

When the ducks are cold, cut away the breast meat in one piece without removing the wings, and loosen the legs. With scissors, cut out the breast bones to form a cavity. Pile the stuffing into the cavity, then slice the breasts of the ducks in neat diagonal slices and arrange them on top of the stuffing, reshaping the birds. Chill thoroughly.

To finish, spoon a layer of cool but still liquid aspic over the ducks, chill until set and repeat the coating. Pour remaining aspic into a shallow pan and chill until set. When it is really firm, cut into diamonds, triangles or other shapes. Coarsely chop pan juices (they should be jelled) and put them in the middle of a platter. Set the ducks on top. Garnish with the aspic shapes and watercress. Serve with spiced apricots.

Spiced Apricots

3 lb apricots
2½ cups distilled vinegar
12–18 cloves
two 3 inch pieces cinnamon
  stick
8 allspice berries
4 cups sugar

Method
Bring vinegar and spices, tied together in a cheesecloth, to a boil in a large shallow pan. Add sugar and dissolve slowly without boiling.

Pour boiling water over apricots, let stand 15 seconds, drain and peel them. Cut in half, twist gently and remove the pits. Bring vinegar mixture to a boil and add apricots, rounded side down. Simmer for 15–20 minutes or until very tender.

Lift fruit out of pan with a slotted spoon and into serving dish. Boil liquid hard for 3 minutes or until syrupy, remove spice bag before pouring liquid over apricots.

Caramel Basket

1½ cups sugar
¾ cup water
large pinch of cream of tartar

Marble slab or baking sheet;
  6–7 inch fluted cake pan or
  bowl (2 quart capacity)

This basket may be filled with petits fours or ice cream but, if using ice cream, chill it in the refrigerator first.

Method
Oil the marble slab or baking sheet and the outside of the cake pan or bowl. Heat sugar with water until sugar dissolves and stir in the cream of tartar. Bring to a boil and boil rapidly until the syrup is a golden caramel. Stop the boiling at once by dipping the bottom of the pan in cold water. Pour the caramel in a steady stream onto the oiled marble slab or baking sheet and let stand for 1–2 minutes or until it begins to set.

Turn the oiled cake pan or the bowl upside down. When the caramel is set but still warm and pliable, loosen it with an oiled spatula, lift it onto the oiled pan or bowl and gently mold it with your hands, curling edges to flute them. Let stand until hard – about 5 minutes. Lift onto a wire rack or lightly oiled plate.

Golden Fruit Gelatin

1 can (15 oz) sliced mangoes, drained
1 can (11 oz) mandarin oranges, drained
2 ripe peaches, peeled, pitted and sliced
4 cups cool but still liquid lemon gelatin, or 2 packages prepared lemon gelatine
1 cup heavy cream, stiffly whipped (for serving) – optional

Ring mold (2 quart capacity)

Serves 8 people.

Method
Pour enough lemon gelatin into the ring mold to cover the bottom to a depth of $\frac{1}{2}$ inch and chill until set.

Arrange a layer of sliced mangoes on the lemon gelatin in the bottom of the mold, pour over just enough cool gelatin to cover and chill until set. Add a layer of mandarin oranges, cover with gelatin and chill until set. Add a layer of peach slices, cover with more gelatin and chill until set. Continue layering the fruit until the mold is full, ending with a layer of lemon gelatin. Cover and chill at least 2 hours or until set.

To serve, dip the mold quickly in warm water, then turn out onto a platter. If you like, fill the center with stiffly whipped cream.

Croquembouche

For French flan pastry (for base)
scant $\frac{1}{2}$ cup flour
2 tablespoons butter
2 tablespoons sugar
1 egg yolk
$\frac{1}{2}$ teaspoon vanilla

For choux pastry (for cream puffs)
$\frac{2}{3}$ cup water
$\frac{1}{3}$ cup butter
$\frac{2}{3}$ cup flour
3–4 eggs

For filling
Chantilly cream (made with 1 cup heavy cream, stiffly whipped and flavored with 1 tablespoon sugar and $\frac{1}{2}$ teaspoon vanilla), or 2 cups vanilla-flavored pastry cream (see page 65)

To finish
1 egg, beaten to mix with $\frac{1}{2}$ teaspoon salt (for glaze)
$\frac{1}{4}$ cup slivered almonds, very finely chopped (for topping)
2–3 tablespoons confectioners' sugar (for sprinkling)
few candied cherries, halved, or pieces of angelica (for decoration)

For syrup
$\frac{1}{2}$ cup sugar
$\frac{1}{3}$ cup water
small pinch of cream of tartar

Pastry bag; $\frac{3}{8}$ inch plain tube and small plain tube

This is a decorative dessert that makes a spectacular centerpiece for a buffet. The cream puffs may be filled with Chantilly cream or vanilla-flavored pastry cream and decorated with spun sugar. Serves 8–10 people.

Method
Make the French flan pastry dough and chill it 30 minutes.

Set oven at moderately hot (375°F).

Roll the French flan dough into a neat 8-inch circle, using a flan ring or plate as a guide. Prick the dough well and bake in heated oven for 15 minutes or until golden brown. Transfer to a wire rack to cool. Turn the oven up to hot (400°F).

Make the choux pastry dough, pipe onto a dampened baking sheet into small even-sized balls, using a pastry bag fitted with the three-eighths inch plain tube. Brush the balls lightly with egg glaze, top each with pinch of chopped almonds and sprinkle lightly with confectioners' sugar. Bake them in the heated oven 10 minutes, then increase heat to 425°F and bake 10–20 minutes longer (depending on their size) or until firm and crisp. Transfer puffs to a wire rack to cool.

Make a slit in the side of each puff and, using the pastry bag fitted with the small plain tube, fill the puffs with Chantilly cream or pastry cream.

To make the syrup: heat half the sugar with half the water in a saucepan until dissolved. Add a small pinch of cream of tartar, then boil rapidly until the syrup is a pale golden caramel (310°F–312°F on a sugar thermometer). Stop the boiling by dipping bottom of the pan in cold water, then tilt pan by lifting one side onto a cloth.

Take a cream puff in one hand, dip the flat side into the syrup and attach to the circle of French flan pastry, leaving about $\frac{1}{2}$ inch around the edge. Then take another cream puff and repeat the process, attaching it so that the puffs touch each other. Continue until there is a complete ring formed on the pastry. Build another ring on top of the first one, angling it slightly in from the edge to make a smaller circle.

Watchpoint: when the sugar syrup gets too firm, warm it to soften but do not reboil or it will crystallize.

When syrup is all used, make a fresh quantity with the remaining sugar and water.

Continue attaching the puffs, adding 4–6 rings and narrowing each circle. Decrease the number of puffs in each ascending ring until top ring leaves a space of about 1–2 inches. Fill the center with one last puff.

Decorate croquembouche with halved candied cherries or angelica, dipping each piece in syrup and letting it set completely before attaching them to the cream puffs with more syrup.

For croquembouche, dip the cream puffs in sugar syrup and attach them next to each other around the pastry shell base

Build up the cream puffs in ascending rings

With more sugar syrup, attach candied fruit decorations between the cream puffs

Gold Cake

3 cups cake flour
3 teaspoons baking powder
1 cup butter
1 cup sugar
grated rind of 1 orange
8 egg yolks
¾ cup milk

For decoration
¾ cup apricot jam glaze (see
   page 53)
2 cup quantity fondant icing
   (see page 52)
1 cup royal icing (see page 53)
yellow food coloring

*10 inch springform pan; plain
   and shell decorating tubes;
   2 paper decorating cones*

Method
Grease the pan and line it with wax paper; grease the paper and sprinkle the pan with flour, discarding the excess.

Set oven at moderate (350°F).

Sift the cake flour and baking powder together several times. Cream the butter until it is soft and light, then gradually add the sugar and orange rind a little at a time, beating thoroughly until the mixture is light and fluffy. Beat in the egg yolks one at a time. With a large metal spoon, fold in the flour mixture alternately with the milk, adding enough milk to keep the batter soft and light.

Pour the batter into the prepared pan, smoothing it over the top with a spatula and hollowing the center slightly. Bake in the heated oven for 1–1¼ hours or until a skewer inserted in the center comes out clean. Cool the cake in the pan for about 10 minutes, then turn out onto a wire rack to cool completely.

When cold, brush cake with apricot jam glaze. Melt the fondant icing and pour it over the cake, spreading it quickly with a spatula; let stand until set. Fill a little royal icing, tinted yellow with food coloring, into the paper cone, fitted with the plain tube, and pipe '50' on top of the cake or the wedding date, if you like. Fill the remaining royal icing into the paper cone, fitted with the shell tube, and pipe a border around the base and edges of the cake.

Top the cake with a golden rose and a butterfly and tie a yellow ribbon around the sides.

A celebration dinner includes œufs d'or (left), boulettes de poulet served with green peas and boiled rice; at back, apricot Moscovite with apricot sauce and chocolate and praline candies

DINNER FOR 12

Oeufs d'Or
(Golden Eggs)

Boulettes de Poulet
(Chicken Balls in
Cream Sauce)

Boiled Rice
French Beans or Peas

Apricot Moscovite

Chocolate
and Praline Candies

TIMETABLE

Day before
Hard cook the eggs; make mayonnaise.
Make apricot Moscovite, cover tightly and chill.
Make chocolate and praline candies.

Morning
Make and bake chicken boulettes and leave in roasting pan for reheating.
Make sauce for chicken but do not add liaison.
Boil rice, drain and leave in buttered dish ready for reheating.
Halve eggs, remove yolks and keep tightly covered.
Arrange whites on platter with mayonnaise and cover tightly. Finish sauce, and keep covered in sauceboat.

Order of Work
7:00
Set oven at moderate (350°F).
Unmold and decorate apricot Moscovite and keep in refrigerator.
7:15
Put chicken boulettes and rice in oven to reheat.
7:30
Cook beans or peas. Finish and garnish eggs.
7:50
Reheat mushroom sauce, add liaison and spoon over boulettes; keep warm.
8:00
Serve eggs.
Reheat beans or peas in butter, just before serving.

Oeufs d'Or
(Golden Eggs)

12 hard-cooked eggs, peeled
$\frac{3}{4}$ cup mayonnaise (see page 86)
2–3 tablespoons sweet chutney or sweet pickle relish, chopped
24 small rounds of buttered wholewheat bread
bunch of watercress (for garnish)

For sauce
$\frac{1}{4}$ cup tomato juice
1 teaspoon curry powder
$1\frac{1}{2}$ cups mayonnaise
2–3 tablespoons sweet chutney or sweet pickle relish, finely chopped
$\frac{1}{4}$–$\frac{1}{3}$ cup heavy cream

Method
Cut the eggs in half lengthwise, scoop out the yolks and work them through a sieve; put the whites in cold water.

Mix the $\frac{3}{4}$ cup mayonnaise with the sweet chutney or pickle relish. Pat the egg whites dry with paper towels and place them on rounds of buttered wholewheat bread on a platter.

Put a little of the mayonnaise mixture into the cavity of each egg white and carefully spoon sieved egg yolk on top.

To make the sauce: mix the tomato juice with the curry powder and stir into the mayonnaise. Add the chutney and enough cream to make a sauce of pouring consistency.

Serve the sauce in a sauceboat and garnish the platter of eggs with watercress just before serving.

Watchpoint: do not complete this dish more than 30 minutes before serving, otherwise the yolks will dry up. Keep the yolks in a covered bowl until you are finishing the dish.

Boulettes de Poulet
(Chicken Balls in Cream Sauce)

4½–5 lb roasting chicken, or fowl
½ lb ground veal
1 medium onion, finely chopped
½ cup butter
2 cups fresh white breadcrumbs
¾ cup grated Parmesan cheese
1½ tablespoons chopped parsley
salt and pepper
2 eggs, beaten to mix
½ cup seasoned flour (made with ½ teaspoon salt and ¼ teaspoon pepper)

For sauce
5 tablespoons butter
5 tablespoons flour
4 cups well-flavored chicken stock (made from the chicken bones and giblets)
½ lb (2 cups) small mushrooms, sliced and sautéed in 2 tablespoons butter

For liaison
3 egg yolks
1 cup heavy cream

Method
Skin the chicken or fowl, removing any fat, and cut all the meat from the bones. Remove any tendons from the legs and work the meat twice through the fine blade of a grinder.

Set the oven at moderately low (325°F).

Put the ground chicken into a bowl and work it well with the ground veal.

Cook the onion in 2 tablespoons butter until soft but not brown. Add to the ground chicken with the breadcrumbs, cheese and parsley. Season the mixture well and mix thoroughly with enough beaten egg to bind. Shape into walnut-sized balls and roll them in seasoned flour.

In a large skillet heat the remaining butter and fry the balls for about 5 minutes or until they are a light golden brown on all sides. Fry them in 2–3 batches, if necessary.

Transfer the balls carefully to a large roasting pan, cover tightly with foil and bake in heated oven for 40–45 minutes.

To make the sauce: in a pan melt the butter, stir in the flour and cook until pale straw-colored. Take from the heat, pour in the stock and bring to a boil, stirring constantly. Season and simmer sauce until it is the consistency of heavy cream. Mix the egg yolks and cream for liaison, stir in a little of the hot sauce and add to the remaining sauce with the sautéed mushrooms. Reheat carefully, stirring until the sauce thickens slightly, but do not boil. Keep the sauce warm in a water bath until ready to serve.

When the boulettes are cooked, spoon them into a deep serving dish, strain any juices from the roasting pan into the sauce and taste for seasoning. Coat the boulettes generously with sauce and serve with boiled rice and buttered green beans or peas.

Apricot Moscovite

To serve 8–12 people, make twice the quantity given in Volume 14 and use 2 molds, each 5 cup capacity.

For apricot Moscovite, pipe rosettes of whipped cream on top of mold

Chocolate and Praline Candies

6 squares (6 oz) semisweet chocolate, chopped
2 tablespoons butter
½ teaspoon vanilla, or 1 teaspoon brandy
praline powder, made with 3 tablespoons whole, unblanched almonds and 3 tablespoons sugar (see page 53)

1–1½ inch cookie cutter

Makes 24–30 candies.

Method
Melt the chocolate in a bowl over a pan of hot water, taking care not to heat the chocolate too much. Take the pan from the heat and work in the butter, vanilla or brandy

Children's pussyfoot cocktail

and the praline powder, a little at a time. Spread the mixture about one-eighth inch thick on wax paper and let stand in a cool place (not in the refrigerator) until almost set. Cut mixture into $1-1\frac{1}{2}$ inch rounds or squares. Chill the candies until hard and peel off the wax paper; store in an airtight container.

DRINKS

For so memorable an occasion featuring sumptuous food, no wine will do so well as Champagne, and if the sky's the limit you might choose one of the rare vintages. These highest quality Champagnes are given extra time to mature and, therefore, fetch a high price.

If your anniversary party is to be very large, vintage Champagne may not be appropriate; in this case select any of the standard editions from the Champagne district in France or a similar sparkling wine from New York or California.

Champagne Cocktail

For each glass
$\frac{1}{8}$ bottle chilled Champagne
2–3 drops of brandy
1 sugar cube
slice of orange

Method
Drop the brandy onto the cube of sugar in the Champagne glass, fill with chilled Champagne and add a slice of orange.

Buck's Fizz

Half fill each Champagne glass with orange juice and pour in an equal amount of chilled Champagne.

Apricot and Orange Cup

2 cans (12 oz each) or 1 can (24 oz) apricot nectar
1 can (6 oz) frozen orange juice
2 quarts club soda
ice cubes

Serves 12–15.

Method
Two or three hours before serving, transfer frozen orange juice from the freezer to the refrigerator. Just before serving, mix all the ingredients together and pour over ice in a punch bowl.

Children's Pussyfoot Cocktail

For each glass
3 tablespoons fresh orange juice
$\frac{1}{2}$ cup bitter lemon soda
slice of orange
long strands of orange rind (for decoration) – optional

Method
Mix the soda with the orange juice and add a slice of orange. Decorate the glass with a strand of orange rind, if you like.

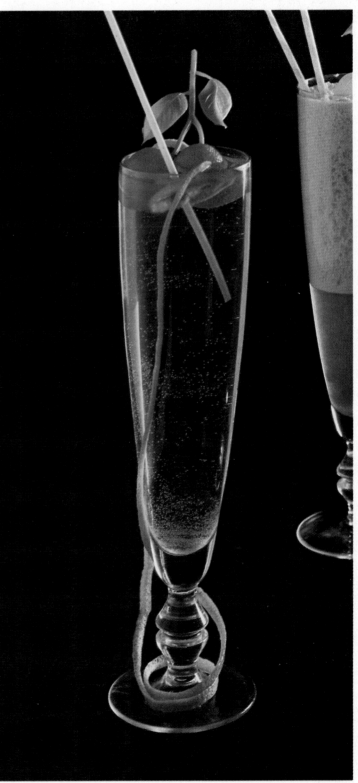

111

Cassata is a popular iced dessert (recipe is on page 117)

112

BOMBES, PARFAITS AND ICED DESSERTS

Few desserts have more universal appeal than a many-layered parfait topped with cream or a molded bombe that hides within its ample curves the surprise of multi-flavored ice cream stripes.

Bombes are named for the traditional bomb-shaped molds that are almost spherical with a flat bottom. They were made that way so the mold was easy to bury in the ice and salt needed to keep the ice cream cold, though now they are usually stored in the freezer. Any deep, plain mold can be used instead of a bombe mold — a melon mold or a plain stainless steel bowl is particularly suitable.

For a bombe, one kind of ice cream can be used to fill the mold, or a combination of ice cream, sherbet or parfait of different flavors can be layered on the bottom and sides of the mold so that the bombe is striped when cut in wedges like a cake. The center of a bombe may be filled simply with whipped cream mixed with candied fruit or shaved chocolate, or with a special egg mousse mixture in a variety of flavors.

Parfaits are delicate and rich, made with an egg mousse base flavoring and lightly whipped cream. The mixture needs no stabilizer to keep it smooth and is not churned or beaten during freezing. Often parfait mixtures are layered with meringues or ladyfingers, soaked in liqueur, to add a contrast of flavor and texture. Large parfaits are usually molded and turned out for serving, but individual parfaits look most attractive when they are frozen in layers in clear glasses so the layers can be seen. They can also be frozen in ramekins or individual soufflé dishes. The consistency of a parfait should be just firm enough to hold its shape, not stiff like ice cream.

'Coupe' means simply cup, and when used for iced desserts the term means a combination of ice cream and fruit, garnished with cream, candied fruit or flowers or chopped nuts, and served in a glass or silver cup. Sundaes, the American version of coupes, are similar but always have sauces added.

Be sure to read the general instructions on ice cream and sherbet in Volume 11 before you begin.

Points to remember

1 Traditional bombe molds are made of tin-lined copper to conduct the heat well. They have a screw or cork at the top of the sphere to release the air-lock so that the ice cream is easy to turn out. Any deep mold such as a charlotte mold, melon mold, stainless steel bowl or a cake pan can be used instead but the sides should be relatively smooth because ice cream molded in complicated patterns does not turn out well.

2 To fill the mold, chill it with the lid. Freeze the ice cream until it is very stiff but not so firm that it cannot be shaped. Spoon it into the chilled mold, pressing down well so no air pockets are left.

3 Often recipes call for 2 or more mixtures to be layered in the same mold. To do this, line the mold about 1 inch thick with stiff ice cream, hollowing the center, and chill until firm. Add another layer, chill again and continue adding layers until the mold is filled to the brim. Level the top with a knife, cover it with wax paper and add the lid or wrap the mold tightly in foil and then freeze it.

4 If the mold is to be stored in ice, a tight-fitting lid is essential. Seal the space between lid and mold with shortening to prevent any salt from entering and bury the mold in a mixture of 3 parts ice to 1 part rock salt. To hold the ice, any regular bucket will do, or use the bucket of a churn freezer. Cover the bucket with a thick cloth or newspaper. During freezing drain off any water and add more ice and salt as necessary. A mold can also be stored in the refrigerator freezing compartment with the control turned to maximum cold or in the freezer.

5 To be sure the mixture is firm before turning out, keep a bombe or parfait at least 2–3 hours in ice and salt or in the freezer.

6 To turn out molded ice cream and parfait mixtures set in cake pans or ice cube trays; chill a platter, preferably made of silver or stainless steel. Dip the cake pan or ice tray for 5 seconds in a deep bowl of cold water; 2 dippings should be enough to loosen the mixture. Dry the pan or ice tray and remove the foil. Turn it upside down onto the platter; the mixture should slide out easily. If not, wrap a warm cloth around the mold.

7 To turn out a bombe: follow the method above, but dip once in the cold water. Dry and remove the lid, replace it but not tightly, and dip again in cold water up to the level of the lid. After the second dipping, dry again and remove the lid and wax paper. Continue as above, loosening the screw at the top of the mold.

8 To finish, decorate the mold with a piped border of stiffly whipped cream or spoon a chilled sauce of contrasting color around it — Melba, apricot or chocolate sauces are particularly suitable.

Note: all **ice cream** and **sherbet** recipes needed for these **desserts** were given in Volume 11, except for **peppermint ice cream** which was given in Volume 16.

Basic Mousse Mixture for Bombes

Beat 3 egg yolks until slightly thickened. Heat $\frac{1}{3}$ cup sugar with $\frac{1}{3}$ cup water until dissolved, bring to a boil and cook until the syrup forms a thread between finger and thumb when a little is lifted on a spoon ($230°F - 234°F$ on a sugar thermometer). Let the bubbles subside, then gradually add the hot syrup to the egg yolks, beating constantly. Continue beating the mixture until it is cool, thick and light, then set bowl over ice and beat until chilled. Stir in the flavoring called for in the recipe, then fold in 1 cup heavy cream, whipped until fairly stiff.

Chocolate Bombe

1 pint chocolate ice cream
1 pint orange sherbet or
   1 pint peppermint ice cream
   chocolate caraque (see page 68)
1 cup heavy cream, stiffly whipped
2 tablespoons Grand Marnier or crème de methe

For decoration
1 cup heavy cream, stiffly whipped
candied violets

Bombe mold or stainless steel bowl ($1\frac{1}{2}$ quart capacity); pastry bag; medium star tube

Serves 8 people.

Method
Freeze ice creams or sherbet until they are firm but can still be shaped; chill mold or bowl. Fold chocolate caraque into whipped cream with Grand Marnier if using orange sherbet, or crème de menthe if using peppermint ice cream.

To fill mold or bowl: line with 1 inch layer of chocolate ice cream and freeze until firm; add orange sherbet or peppermint ice cream to make an inner layer; freeze again until firm. Fill center with liqueur-flavored cream, cover with wax paper, seal in foil and freeze.

To serve, unmold bombe onto a chilled platter and, using pastry bag fitted with the star tube, coat with rosettes of whipped cream. Stud cream with candied violets and serve.

Coffee Bombe

Line the bottom and sides of 1 quart bombe mold or stainless steel bowl with 1 pint coffee ice cream and chill until set; then fill with basic mousse mixture, flavored with 3 tablespoons brandy. Chill.

Turn out and decorate bombe with rosettes of whipped cream, studded with a few candied rose petals.

To Make a Bombe in a Mold

Seal the space between the lid and the bombe mold with shortening, then cover the mold with wax paper and lid

Loosen the screw at the top of the mold before turning out the bombe

Bury the filled mold in the ice and rock salt mixture

Bombe Véronique

Line the bottom and sides of a 1½ quart bombe mold or stainless steel bowl with 1 pint pistachio ice cream. Chill until set; then add 1 pint chocolate chip ice cream to make an inner layer. Chill until set, then fill with basic mousse mixture, flavored with 2 oz melted sweet chocolate. Chill until firm. Turn out; decorate with whipped cream rosettes and chocolate rounds (see Index). Serves 8 people.

Strawberry Bombe

Line the bottom and sides of a 1½ quart bombe mold or stainless steel bowl with 1 pint strawberry ice cream and freeze until firm. Then add 1 pint raspberry sherbet to make an inner layer. Chill until firm, then fill the center with basic mousse mixture, flavored with ¼ cup praline powder (see page 53) and chill. Turn out and decorate the bombe with strawberry halves sprinkled with kirsch, or coat with rosettes of whipped cream and stud with candied violets. Serve with strawberry custard sauce, if you like. Serves 8.

Strawberry Custard Sauce

Make 3 cups crème a la vanille (see Index); flavor with 1 tablespoon kirsch or lemon juice and strawberry purée (work 1 cup fresh or frozen strawberries through a sieve or purée in a blender).

Strawberry bombe is decorated with rosettes of cream and candied violets and served with strawberry custard sauce (recipe is on page 115)

Meringue Glacé Maison 1

½ cup candied ginger
1½ cups heavy cream, stiffly
   whipped

For meringue
3 egg whites
¾ cup sugar

For white coffee ice cream
1½ cups light cream
½ cup whole coffee beans
1 egg
1 egg yolk
¼ cup sugar
1 cup heavy cream, whipped
   until it holds a soft shape

For decoration (optional)
½ cup heavy cream, stiffly
   whipped
1–2 slices of candied ginger,
   cut in slivers

*Silicone paper; 7–8 inch
springform pan (2½ quart
capacity); pastry bag; ⅜ inch
plain tube; star tube
(optional)*

This recipe consists of layers
of ice cream and meringue
molded in a cake pan. The
white coffee ice cream is
flavored with coffee beans,
with no extra coffee flavoring
added. Serves 10–12 people.

Method
Line 3 baking sheets with silicone paper and mark 5–6 inch
circles on them. Set oven at
low (250°F). Chill the springform pan.
   To make the meringue:
beat the egg whites until they
hold a stiff peak, add 1 tablespoon sugar and beat 1
minute longer or until the
mixture is glossy. Fold in the
remaining sugar with a metal
spoon. Divide the mixture
evenly between the 3 baking
sheets and spread it to 5–6
inch circles or put into the

pastry bag fitted with the plain
tube and pipe the meringue in
circles on the sheets.
   Bake the rounds in the
heated oven for about 1 hour
or until they are cream-colored
and crisp. Let cool slightly,
then peel off the paper and let
cool completely on a rack.
   To make the white coffee
ice cream: scald the light
cream with coffee beans.
Cover and infuse over very
low heat for 15 minutes or
until milk is well flavored and
pale coffee-colored. Beat egg
and egg yolk with the sugar
until light and slightly thick,
strain in the scalded cream
and beat well until mixed.
Strain again and let cool.
Stir in the lightly whipped
cream, chill thoroughly, then
freeze in a churn freezer or in
a bucket of ice and salt for
about 3 hours or until firm.
   Pour boiling water over the
candied ginger, let stand 15
minutes, then drain and chop
it. Fold it into the stiffly
whipped cream.
   To fill the springform pan:
line the chilled pan with a 1
inch layer of white coffee ice
cream, using the back of a
spoon to smooth the mixture.
Set a round of cold meringue
on top and cover with a layer
of the ginger and cream
mixture. Add a layer of
meringue, then the remaining
ginger cream mixture. Top
with the last meringue round
and fill mold with ice cream,
packing it into the space at
the sides. Cover with wax
paper, wrap securely in foil
and freeze. If freezing for more
than 12 hours, transfer to the
refrigerator 1–2 hours before
serving, then unmold onto a
chilled platter. If you like,
using the pastry bag fitted
with the star tube, decorate
the meringue glacé with
rosettes of whipped cream
and top them with slivers of
candied ginger.

Meringue Glacé Maison 2

In the recipe left, substitute 1 quart chocolate ice
cream for white coffee ice
cream. Use ½ cup chopped
canned kumquats, drained,
instead of the candied ginger.
Do not scald the kumquats.

Cassata

1 pint vanilla ice cream
1 pint chocolate ice cream
¾ cup heavy cream, stiffly
   whipped
½ cup mixed chopped candied
   fruit
2 tablespoons rum

*Bombe mold or stainless steel
bowl (1½ quart capacity)*

Serves 8 people.

Method
Mix the candied fruit with the
rum and let macerate 30 minutes. Freeze the ice creams
until they are firm but can
still be shaped; chill the mold
or bowl.
   To fill the mold or bowl: line
the bottom and sides with a
1 inch layer of vanilla ice
cream, freeze until firm, then
add the chocolate ice cream
to make an inner layer and
freeze until firm. Fold the
candied fruit into the whipped
cream and pile into the center
of the mold. Cover with wax
paper, wrap securely in foil
and freeze.
   To serve, unmold cassata
onto a chilled platter and cut
in wedges.

Coupe Jacques

¾ pint lemon sherbet
¾ pint strawberry sherbet
2 cups mixed fresh fruits such
   as halved strawberries;
   orange sections; pared,
   sliced pear; seedless grapes;
   sliced banana; cubed
   pineapple
2 tablespoons kirsch
4 candied cherries, halved
2 tablespoons whole blanched
   almonds, split and browned

4 sherbet glasses

Method
Mix the fruits with 1 tablespoon kirsch, cover and let
macerate in refrigerator 1–2
hours; chill the glasses.
   To serve, place a scoop of
lemon and strawberry sherbet
on each side of the glasses
and spoon the macerated fruit
down the center. Sprinkle
with remaining kirsch, top
each scoop of sherbet with a
halved cherry and scatter with
split almonds.

Note: when **chilling glass
serving dishes** or **cups**,
do not leave them in the
freezer or refrigerator too
long or they may crack.
**When freezing parfaits
in glasses**, use heat
resistant glasses.

Coupe Suzette

1 pint fresh raspberries or
   1 package frozen raspberries,
   drained
$1\frac{1}{2}$ pints pistachio ice cream
1 tablespoon kirsch
Chantilly cream, made with
   1 cup heavy cream, stiffly
   whipped and flavored with
   3–4 teaspoons sugar,
   $\frac{1}{2}$ teaspoon vanilla
$\frac{1}{4}$ cup green maraschino
   cherries, drained and finely
   chopped

*4 sherbet glasses; pastry bag
and small star tube*

Method
Sprinkle the kirsch over the raspberries and let macerate 10 minutes; chill the glasses.

To serve: place a large scoop of pistachio ice cream in the center of each glass and surround with the raspberries. Cover raspberries and ice cream completely with rosettes of Chantilly cream, using a pastry bag fitted with a small star tube. Sprinkle the cream with finely chopped maraschino cherries and serve.

Peach Parfait

3–4 fresh peaches or 6–8
   canned peach halves, drained
4 large macaroons, crushed
3–4 tablespoons kirsch
$\frac{1}{2}$ cup sugar
$\frac{1}{3}$ cup water
2 egg whites
$\frac{1}{4}$ teaspoon almond extract
$1\frac{1}{2}$ cups heavy cream, whipped
   until it holds a soft shape
$\frac{1}{2}$ cup heavy cream, stiffly
   whipped (for decoration)

*6–8 parfait glasses, or 9 inch
springform pan*

Serves 6–8 people.

Method
Scald fresh peaches, peel, halve and discard the pits. Work them or canned peaches through a sieve or purée them in a blender. Measure the purée – there should be 2 cups. Chill purée and parfait glasses or springform pan. Sprinkle kirsch over the crushed macaroons.

Heat the sugar with the water until dissolved, bring to a boil and cook until syrup forms a thread between finger and thumb when a little is lifted on a spoon (230°F – 234°F on a sugar thermometer). Stiffly whip the egg whites. Let bubbles subside and pour the hot sugar syrup into the egg whites, beating constantly. Continue beating until this meringue is cool and thick.

Fold the meringue into peach purée with the almond extract, then fold in the lightly whipped cream. Spoon about one-third of the mixture into the chilled glasses or pan and spread with half the macaroon mixture. Continue adding layers until both peach mixture and macaroons are used, ending with peach mixture. Cover with wax paper, wrap the springform pan in foil and freeze.

To serve, using the pastry bag fitted with the star tube, top each glass of parfait with a rosette of whipped cream, or turn out the molded parfait onto a chilled platter and surround with a piped border of whipped cream.

Coffee Parfait

4 egg yolks
2 tablespoons dry instant
   coffee
$\frac{1}{3}$ cup sugar
$\frac{1}{3}$ cup water
1 cup light cream and $1\frac{1}{2}$ cups
   heavy cream or $2\frac{1}{2}$ cups
   heavy cream

For decoration (optional)
$\frac{3}{4}$ cup heavy cream, stiffly
   whipped
10–12 chocolate coffee bean
   candies

*Bombe mold (5 cup capacity)
or 8–9 inch cake pan; pastry
bag and medium star tube
(optional)*

Serves 6 people.

Method
If using a cake pan, line it with a circle of foil; chill the bombe mold or pan.

Beat the egg yolks with the instant coffee until slightly thickened. Heat the sugar with the water until dissolved, bring to a boil and cook until the syrup forms a thread between finger and thumb when a little is lifted on a spoon (234°F on a sugar thermometer). Let the bubbles subside, then gradually pour the hot syrup into the egg yolks, beating constantly. Continue beating until the mixture is cool and thick and light. Stir in the light cream or 1 cup heavy cream, if using only heavy cream. Whip the remaining heavy cream until it holds a soft shape and fold it into the coffee mousse.

Pour the mousse mixture into the chilled mold or pan, cover with wax paper and add the lid or seal the pan with foil. Freeze.

To serve: unmold the parfait onto a chilled platter. If using a bombe mold, leave it plain or decorate the base with a border of whipped cream, using a pastry bag fitted with a star tube. If using a cake pan, decorate the top of the parfait with rosettes of whipped cream and top them with chocolate coffee bean candies.

Alternative presentation
Make the coffee parfait mixture as above and pour it into 4 tall stemmed glasses or parfait glasses. Cover tightly and freeze. To serve, top each parfait with a rosette of whipped cream and pour over 1 tablespoon Tia Maria coffee liqueur, if you like.

Coffee parfait is topped with rosettes of cream, and coffee-flavored liqueur poured over

Maple Parfait

½ cup maple syrup
2 tablespoons butter
4 eggs, separated
pinch of salt
2 cups heavy cream, whipped
    until it holds a soft shape
½ cup chopped pecans
1 teaspoon vanilla

For decoration
½ cup heavy cream, stiffly
    whipped
8–10 walnut or pecan halves

*6–8 stemmed parfait glasses
or individual soufflé dishes;
pastry bag and medium star
tube*

Serves 6–8 people.

Method
Chill the glasses or tie paper collars around the soufflé dishes and chill.

In the top of a double boiler heat the maple syrup with the butter until very hot. Stir the egg yolks until mixed and gradually beat them into the maple syrup mixture. Take from the heat and continue beating until the mixture is cool and light and thick. Stiffly whip the egg whites with a pinch of salt and fold into the maple mixture with the lightly whipped cream, chopped pecans and vanilla. Spoon the mixture into the chilled glasses or soufflé dishes, cover with wax paper and freeze.

To serve: using a pastry bag and medium star tube, pipe a rosette of whipped cream on top of each parfait and top with a halved walnut or pecan.

Rêve de Bébé
(Baby's Dream)

2 tablespoons orange juice
1 pint small fresh strawberries,
    hulled
1 pint pineapple sherbet
1 pint raspberry ice cream or
    sherbet
½ cup heavy cream, stiffly
    whipped
few candied violets (optional)

*4 sherbet glasses; pastry bag
and small star tube*

Method
Sprinkle the orange juice over the strawberries and let macerate 10 minutes; chill the glasses.

To serve: place scoops of pineapple and raspberry ice cream or sherbet on each side of the glasses and arrange the strawberries between them. Pipe small rosettes of whipped cream around each glass, using a pastry bag fitted with a small star tube, and, if you like, sprinkle the cream with candied violets.

Strawberries Jeanne Granier

1 quart strawberries, hulled
2–3 tablespoons Curaçao,
    Grand Marnier or other
    orange liqueur
2–3 tablespoons confectioners'
    sugar (or to taste)
1 quart orange sherbet

For orange liqueur mousse
3 egg yolks
⅓ cup sugar
½ cup water
2–3 tablespoons Curaçao,
    Grand Marnier or other
    orange liqueur
1 cup heavy cream, whipped
    until fairly stiff

Glass bowl (4 quart capacity)

Serves 8 people.

Method
Sprinkle the strawberries with orange liqueur and sugar to taste; cover and let macerate in the refrigerator.

To make the mousse: beat the egg yolks until slightly thickened. Heat the sugar with the water until dissolved, bring to a boil and cook until the syrup forms a thread between finger and thumb when a little is lifted on a spoon (230°F − 234°F on a sugar thermometer). Let the bubbles subside, then gradually add the hot syrup to the egg yolks, beating constantly. Continue beating until the mixture is cool, thick and light, then set the bowl over ice and continue beating until chilled. Stir in orange liqueur, followed by the whipped cream.

Set the glass bowl over a large bowl of cracked ice and spread orange sherbet in the bottom. Spoon over the strawberries with their juice and pile the orange liqueur mousse on top. Serve at once.

For strawberries Jeanne Granier, orange mousse is piled on top of strawberries, soaked in orange liqueur, with a layer of orange sherbet in the bottom

Chocolate truffles are given an even coating of melted chocolate and cocoa. They are delicious with demitasse coffee

122

CHOCOLATE TRUFFLES COMPLETE A GOURMET MENU

Consommé Madrilène

Capon à la Crème
Mashed Potatoes   Green Salad

Strawberry Orange Sherbet
with Fours aux Amandes
(Almond Petits Fours)

Chocolate Truffles

Red wine (for capon) – Margaux (Médoc)
or Cabernet Sauvignon (California)
White wine (for dessert) – Barsac (Sauternes)
or Sweet Sauvignon Blanc (California)

This menu of your Grand Diplôme Cooking Course is simple but superb – a delicate consommé Madrilène, followed by a plump capon resplendent with a cream sauce, then a sherbet of fresh strawberries with petits fours. Chocolate truffles will make demitasse coffee especially delicious.

For this succulent capon only the most elegant and subtle red wine will do, so choose a Margaux from France's Médoc district. If there is an American contender, it is a well-aged Cabernet Sauvignon from one of the premier vineyards of California's Napa Valley. The lofty standard established by the reds can be carried on through dessert by serving a brilliant sweet French white wine from Barsac. The closest American counterpart is a Sweet Sauvignon Blanc from California's Napa Valley.

TIMETABLE

Day before
Clarify the consommé (make the stock the previous day) or make the quick consommé.
Make and bake almond petits fours and store in an airtight container.
Make chocolate truffles and store in an airtight container.
Make strawberry orange sherbet and store in freezer.

Morning
Peel potatoes and keep in cold water.
If serving salad, wash salad greens and keep in plastic bag in refrigerator; make dressing.
Make béchamel sauce for capon and cover tightly.

Assemble ingredients for final cooking from 6 p.m. for dinner around 8 p.m.

Order of Work

6:00
Start cooking capon.
Arrange petits fours and chocolate truffles on dishes for serving.

7:30
Boil potatoes.
Broil or fry the bacon.

7:40
Transfer capon to platter and keep warm. Purée onion and béchamel sauce, finish sauce and spoon over capon, keep warm.

7:50
Heat consommé.
Mash potatoes and keep warm with a layer of milk on top.

8:00
Add extra sherry, if using, to consommé and serve.
Toss salad with dressing and beat milk into mashed potatoes just before serving.
Scoop strawberry orange sherbet into balls just before serving.

> You will find that **cooking times** given in the individual recipes for these dishes have sometimes been adapted in the timetable to help you when cooking and serving this menu as a party meal.

Appetizer

Consommé Madrilène

6 cups well-flavored chicken stock, free from fat
¾ lb boneless shin of beef, finely shredded
¼ cup sherry or Madeira
3 ripe tomatoes, peeled, sliced and seeded
2 teaspoons tomato paste (optional)
salt and pepper
whites and shells (wiped and crushed) of 2 eggs
2–3 tablespoons sherry (optional) – for serving
1 tomato, peeled, seeded and cut in fine strips (for garnish)

Method
Put the stock in a thick enamel, stainless steel or tin-lined kettle with the beef, sherry or Madeira. Add the tomatoes, with tomato paste if fresh tomatoes lack color. Taste the soup for seasoning – it should be strong and well-flavored.

Watchpoint: seasoning must not be added after clarifying liquid with the egg whites as it will cloud the soup.

Whip the egg whites to a light froth and add to the liquid with the crushed shells. Whisk backwards over moderate heat until the liquid boils. Stop whisking and let the liquid rise to the top of the pan. Draw it aside for about 5 minutes, then carefully boil it again, taking care not to break up the 'filter' that forms

Consommé Madrilène is flavored with sherry and tomato

on the top. Lower the heat and leave to simmer very slowly for 40 minutes to extract all the flavor from the meat.

Place a scalded dish towel over a bowl and pour the liquid through; keep the 'filter' back with a spoon at first, then at the end slide it out onto the cloth. The consommé should be clear; if it is not, pour it again through the cloth.

Reheat the consommé before serving but do not let it boil. Taste and add extra sherry if you like, and the strips of tomato.

Consommé Madrilène
(Quick Version)

4 cups well-flavored chicken stock
3 ripe tomatoes, quartered and seeded
4 tablespoons sherry
salt and pepper

Method
Put the tomatoes in a large pan, add 2 tablespoons sherry and the stock, cover and simmer 10–15 minutes or until the tomatoes are soft and pulpy. Draw the pan aside and let stand 15–20 minutes to extract the flavors. Taste for seasoning, strain the soup carefully through scalded cheesecloth and reheat without boiling. Add the remaining sherry if you like, before serving the consommé.

To clarify liquid for consommé, whisk egg white and stock mixture over moderate heat

When the liquid boils, stop whisking and let it rise to the top of the pan

Capon, resplendent with cream sauce, is garnished with crispy slices of bacon

Have ingredients at hand before starting capon à la crème

Entrée

Capon à la Crème

5–6 lb capon
$\frac{1}{4}$ cup unsalted butter
2 Bermuda or other mild
    onions, sliced and blanched
$\frac{1}{3}$ cup brandy
$\frac{1}{2}$–$\frac{3}{4}$ cup chicken stock
béchamel sauce, made with
    2 tablespoons butter,
    2 tablespoons flour, 1$\frac{1}{2}$ cups
    milk (infused with slice of
    onion, 6 peppercorns, blade
    of mace and bay leaf)
$\frac{1}{2}$–1 cup heavy cream
salt and pepper

For garnish
8–10 slices of bacon

Method

Melt the butter in a flame-proof casserole, add the capon, cover the pan and cook very gently for 10–12 minutes until the bird turns white – this is known as 'whitening in butter'. Turn the bird occasionally so it cooks evenly but do not let it brown. Remove the bird from the pan, add the onions, cover and cook 4–5 minutes so the onions soften without browning and absorb the remaining butter. Replace the capon in the pan, pour in the brandy and $\frac{1}{2}$ cup stock. Cover and cook over a low heat on top of the stove or bake in a moderate oven (350°F) for about 1$\frac{1}{2}$ hours or until the capon is tender.

Watchpoint: if cooking the bird on top of the stove, add extra stock if the pan gets dry.

To prepare the bacon garnish: cut slices of bacon in half and broil or fry them until crisp. Drain on paper towels.

Remove capon from the pan, place on a warm platter and keep warm.

Work the onion mixture with the béchamel sauce through a sieve, or purée the onions and sauce in a blender. Pour into a saucepan and reheat. Add enough heavy cream to the sauce to thin it to a coating consistency, bring just to a boil and taste for seasoning.

Spoon enough sauce over the capon to coat it generously and serve the rest separately. Pile the strips of crisp bacon on one side of the platter. The delicate flavor of this dish is best complemented simply by the bacon garnish and an accompaniment of mashed potatoes. However, green salad or a green vegetable can be served as a separate course.

Dessert

Strawberry Orange Sherbet

1 quart strawberries, hulled
grated rind and juice of
    1 orange
1 cup sugar
2$\frac{1}{2}$ cups water
juice of $\frac{1}{2}$ lemon
1 envelope gelatin (optional)
$\frac{1}{4}$ cup water (optional)
1 egg white

Glass bowl or sherbet glasses

If fresh strawberries are not available, it is best to substitute frozen strawberries without sugar. The sherbet can be made in a churn freezer or in ice cube trays (see Volume 11).

Method

Heat the sugar with the water until dissolved. Bring to a boil and boil until the syrup feels sticky when a little is lifted on a spoon (220°F on a sugar thermometer). Pour into a bowl, add lemon juice and let cool. Crush strawberries well with a fork. Stir in the grated rind and the strained juice of the orange, cover and chill thoroughly.

If freezing in ice cube trays, sprinkle gelatin over $\frac{1}{4}$ cup water and let stand 5 minutes until spongy; dissolve over a pan of hot water and stir into the strawberry purée. Add the cool syrup. Freeze the mixture in a churn freezer or in ice cube trays. When slushy, whip the egg white and add 1 tablespoon of it to the sherbet. Continue freezing until firm; pack down sherbet, cover tightly and store in the freezer or in a bucket of ice and rock salt for 3–4 hours.

Pile scoops of sherbet in a chilled bowl or glasses and serve with fours aux amandes (recipe is on next page).

Fours aux Amandes
(Almond Petits Fours)

$\frac{2}{3}$ cup whole blanched
  almonds, ground
$\frac{1}{3}$ cup sugar
2 egg whites
$\frac{1}{2}$ teaspoon vanilla extract or
  $\frac{1}{4}$ teaspoon almond extract
few blanched almonds split in
  half, or candied cherries cut
  in quarters, or diamonds of
  angelica (for decoration)

For glaze
1 tablespoon sugar
2 tablespoons milk

*Silicone paper; pastry bag;
large star tube*

This recipe for almond petits
fours was first given in Volume

17. Makes 12–14 petits
fours.

Method
Set the oven at moderate
(350°F) and line a baking
sheet with silicone paper.
  Mix the almonds and sugar
and sift them through a coarse
sieve. Beat the egg whites
until they hold a stiff peak
and fold in the almonds and
sugar with vanilla or almond
flavoring.
  Spoon the mixture into the
pastry bag fitted with the star
tube, and pipe flowers,
rosettes or figure eights onto
the lined baking sheet. Decorate with split almonds or
pieces of candied cherry or
angelica and bake in the
heated oven for 15 minutes or
until petits fours are just
beginning to brown.
  To make the glaze: heat
sugar with milk until dissolved
and brush over the petits fours
while they are still hot. Cool,
then peel off the paper before
they are completely cold.

Chocolate Truffles

6 squares (6 oz) semisweet
  chocolate, chopped
$\frac{1}{4}$ cup unsalted butter
2 tablespoons strong black
  coffee
praline powder, made with
  $\frac{1}{2}$ cup whole unblanched
  almonds and $\frac{1}{2}$ cup sugar
  (see page 53)
1 teaspoon brandy or rum
$1\frac{1}{2}$ tablespoons heavy cream

To finish
2 squares (2 oz) semisweet
  chocolate
2–3 tablespoons cocoa

These can be made ahead and
stored, with wax paper between layers, in an airtight
container. The flavor mellows

if the truffles are kept 1–2
weeks. Makes about 30
truffles.

Method
Melt the chocolate in a heatproof bowl over a pan of hot
water, take from the heat and
stir in half the butter a small
piece at a time. Gradually
stir in the coffee, then the
remaining butter, piece by
piece. Stir in the praline
powder, brandy or rum and
then the cream; chill 30 minutes.
  Watchpoint: the mixture
must not be stirred too much
while the cream is being
added or it will be too soft
to shape into balls.
  Put heaped teaspoons of
the mixture one at a time on a
sheet of wax paper. Shape
into balls and chill 2 hours
or until firm.
  To finish, melt the 2–3
squares chocolate on a heatproof plate over a pan of hot
water. Sprinkle the cocoa
onto a sheet of wax paper.
Put 1 teaspoon melted chocolate in the palm of one hand,
roll the truffle in it, then in
the cocoa and transfer to a
clean sheet of wax paper.
Continue until all the truffles
are coated. Make sure, however, that you use only just
enough cocoa to coat them
evenly. When the chocolate
sets it will give the truffles
a crisp coating.

*Fours aux amandes petits
fours are piped in flowers,
rosettes or figure eight shapes
and decorated with candied
cherries, diamonds of angelica
and split almonds*

A gourmet menu

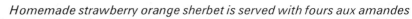

Homemade strawberry orange sherbet is served with fours aux amandes

COOKING WITH FLOWERS

Flowers may seem too frail to survive cooking and are largely ignored as ingredients, but they add fragrance to the flavor of many traditional recipes. Orange flower water, rose water, and a variety of vinegars are the most commonly used cooking ingredients. Fresh woodruff is used to make a drink with sparkling Moselle wine, an aromatic tea, or as a flavoring for cakes and cookies. Violets and rose petals are candied as a decoration for sweet dishes, and rose petals are also used for jams, jellies and vinegars. Verbena goes into fresh fruit salads; sunflower seeds flavor breads, pastries and savory vegetable dishes; and the passion flower combined with fresh peaches, pineapple and banana makes a popular fruit soup in South America.

Cooking with flowers is as old as civilization and today most cuisines of the world have a sprinkling of their own flower recipes. Here are a few.

Pickled Nasturtium Seeds

Pick nasturtium seeds as they become small and green and soak them in brine to cover made from 1 quart water mixed with $\frac{1}{2}$ cup salt. Renew the brine every three days until all the seeds have been collected.

Drain the seeds and pack them in small jars. Pour over enough boiling white wine vinegar to cover, seal and store for about a week before using. Use as a piquant substitute for capers.

Zucchini Flower Fritters

20–24 fresh zucchini blossoms
2 eggs
1 tablespoon water
salt and pepper
about $\frac{3}{4}$ cup flour
deep fat (for frying)

Zucchini flowers (or blossoms) are frequently available in Italian markets during the summer months. They have a delicious, delicate flavor. The flower or blossom of squash and pumpkin may be treated in the same way.

Method
Pick over the blossoms, especially the closed ones, for bugs and bees. Rinse the flowers gently with cold water; they should stay whole.

Beat eggs, water and seasoning together. Dip each blossom in the egg mixture, then sprinkle them lightly with flour. Heat the deep fat to 380°F on a fat thermometer and add a few blossoms at a time. Fry until golden brown, remove with a slotted spoon and drain on paper towels. Keep warm until all the blossoms are cooked, then serve immediately as a vegetable.

Stuffed Squash Blossoms

Many squash blossoms fall off without ever maturing. These are the male blooms and after they close and fall, they make edible cases for stuffings of cooked chicken, veal, clams, oysters and fish.

Open each blossom gently and spoon in just enough stuffing so that the petals still close easily. Arrange the stuffed blossoms side by side in a buttered baking dish, cover with buttered foil and bake them in a moderate oven (350°F) for 15–20 minutes or until the stuffing is very hot. Serve them as a vegetable garnish for roast meat or baked fish.

Rosebud and Carnation Salad

Examine a dozen pink or white rosebuds and pink or white carnations for bugs and bees. Rinse flowers in cold water and cut buds from roses and the petals from carnations, discarding stems. Combine the flowerpetals in a salad bowl with 1 bunch watercress. Shortly before serving, toss with $\frac{1}{4}$ cup vinaigrette dressing made with white wine vinegar and sweetened with a little sugar.

Poetic Salad

Arrange 10–15 washed and dried nasturtium leaves around the outside edge of a salad dish with 10–15 clean nasturtium flowers resting on the leaves, stems pointing toward the center of the dish.

In the middle of the arrangement make a layer of thinly sliced Bermuda or sweet onions, then a layer of 3 peeled and thinly sliced tomatoes and finally a sprinkling of 3 stalks celery, finely chopped. Continue the layers until the dish is filled. Pour $\frac{1}{2}$ cup vinaigrette dressing over the top and sprinkle with 1 finely chopped hard-cooked egg.

Cover and refrigerate for about 3 hours for the nasturtium leaves and flowers to add pungency to the salad.

Pennsylvania Dandelion Salad

4–5 cups dandelion greens, tightly packed
1 small onion, chopped

For bacon dressing
6 strips bacon, diced
2 tablespoons sugar
1 teaspoon flour
1 teaspoon salt
$\frac{1}{4}$ cup vinegar mixed with $\frac{1}{2}$ cup water
1 hard-cooked egg, sliced

Method
For the best flavor and texture, pick dandelion greens while they are young before they bloom. Trim the stems and wash the greens thoroughly in several changes of water; dry them on paper towels and chill in the refrigerator.

To make dressing: fry the bacon in a skillet until almost crisp. Pour off all but 2 table-spoons of the fat and stir in the sugar, flour and salt. Cook over a low heat for about 1 minute. Stir in the vinegar and water and bring to a boil, stirring constantly.

Mix the dandelion greens and onion in a bowl, pour over the dressing while it is still hot and toss well. Garnish with slices of hard-cooked egg.

Elderflower Syrup

Infuse $\frac{1}{2}$ cup washed elderflowers in a sugar and water syrup (made from 1 cup sugar and $\frac{3}{4}$ cup water). Cool and strain into a $\frac{1}{2}$ pint jar. A little added to fresh fruit salad, finished cakes, or strawberries gives a delicious aromatic flavor.

Elderblossom Pancakes

To a $1\frac{1}{2}$ cup quantity regular pancake batter (see Volume 9), stir in $\frac{1}{2}$–$\frac{3}{4}$ cup elderblossoms, pulled from the stems, then washed and dried. Fry the pancakes in butter and when brown on both sides, transfer them to a sheet of wax paper sprinkled with confectioners' sugar. Serve with lemon wedges.

Carnation Marmalade

½ lb fresh red carnation petals
1 cup sugar
1 cup water
½-inch stick cinnamon

Method
Crush carnation petals in a bowl until they are well bruised. Heat sugar, water and cinnamon stick in a saucepan until sugar dissolves. Bring to a boil and boil until syrup spins a thread between finger and thumb when a little is lifted on a spoon (230°F–234°F on a sugar thermometer). Stir in the crushed carnations and continue cooking over a low heat for 8–10 minutes or until the flowers are pulpy. Discard the cinnamon stick, stir the marmalade well and pour it into small dry sterilized glasses; seal at once.

Chrysanthemum Salad

4 chrysanthemums
1 jar (8½ oz) artichoke hearts
1 lb cooked peeled shrimps
3 cooked potatoes, diced
6 hard-cooked eggs, sliced
2 tablespoons capers, drained
salt and pepper
⅓ cup vinaigrette dressing

Method
Cut petals from chrysanthemums, pour boiling water over them, drain thoroughly and cool.

In a salad bowl, combine chrysanthemum petals with the drained artichoke hearts, shrimps, diced potatoes, hard-cooked eggs and drained capers. Toss with vinaigrette dressing, taste for seasoning and serve.

Scrambled Eggs with Marigolds

8 eggs
8 tablespoons milk
salt and pepper
pinch of nutmeg
2 tablespoons butter
petals from 4 marigolds, washed and chopped
4 slices rye bread, toasted and buttered

Method
Beat the egg lightly with milk, seasoning and nutmeg. Melt the butter and scramble the eggs. Just before the eggs are done, stir in the chopped marigold petals. Pile the eggs on the pieces of buttered toast and serve at once.

Rose Geranium Punch

4 cups apple juice
1 cup sugar
6 rose geranium leaves
4 limes, thinly sliced
few drops green food coloring (optional)

Method
Heat apple juice, sugar and rose geranium leaves gently for about 5 minutes without boiling. Stir in sliced limes, crushing them gently with the back of a large spoon. Cool the mixture, strain and add a few drops green food coloring, if you like.

Pour into glasses filled with crushed ice and decorate with a few rose geranium petals.

Waldmeister-bowle
(Woodruff or May Wine)

2 large bunches of fresh woodruff or 1 cup dried woodruff
½ cup superfine (or bar) sugar
2 bottles of sparkling Moselle wine
1 quart fresh strawberries (optional)

This wine cup is traditionally made in May, when fresh woodruff is at its best before it comes into flower. The herb gives a pleasantly aromatic flavor to the wine.

Method
Tie the woodruff with string, place it in a punch bowl and sprinkle over the sugar. Pour over 1 bottle of the wine, cover and stand for ½–1 hour or until the wine is flavored to your taste.

Lift out the fresh woodruff or remove the dried woodruff with a slotted spoon. Add the strawberries, if using, and chill thoroughly. Just before serving, add the remaining bottle of wine.

Note: recipe for vinaigrette dressing is on page 44.

MEASURING & MEASUREMENTS

The recipe quantities in the Course are measured in standard level teaspoons, tablespoons and cups and their equivalents are shown below. Any liquid pints and quarts also refer to U.S. standard measures.

When measuring dry ingredients, fill the cup or spoon to overflowing without packing down and level the top with a knife. All the dry ingredients, including flour, should be measured before sifting, although sifting may be called for later in the instructions.

Butter and margarine usually come in measured sticks (1 stick equals $\frac{1}{2}$ cup) and other bulk fats can be measured by displacement. For $\frac{1}{3}$ cup fat, fill the measuring cup $\frac{2}{3}$ full of water. Add fat until the water reaches the 1 cup mark. Drain the cup of water and the fat remaining equals $\frac{1}{3}$ cup.

For liquids, fill the measure to the brim, or to the calibration line.

Often quantities of seasonings cannot be stated exactly, for ingredients vary in the amount they require. The instructions 'add to taste' are literal, for it is impossible to achieve just the right balance of flavors in many dishes without tasting them.

Liquid measure	Volume equivalent
3 teaspoons	1 tablespoon
2 tablespoons	1 fluid oz
4 tablespoons	$\frac{1}{4}$ cup
16 tablespoons	1 cup or 8 fluid oz
2 cups	1 pint
2 pints	1 quart
4 quarts	1 gallon

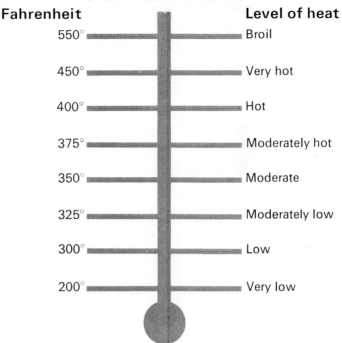

OVEN TEMPERATURES

Fahrenheit		Level of heat
550°		Broil
450°		Very hot
400°		Hot
375°		Moderately hot
350°		Moderate
325°		Moderately low
300°		Low
200°		Very low

OVEN TEMPERATURES AND SHELF POSITIONS

Throughout the Cooking Course, oven temperatures are stated in degrees Fahrenheit and in generally agreed levels of heat such as 'high' and 'moderate'. The equivalents are shown on the table above.

However, exact temperature varies in different parts of an oven and the thermostat reading refers to the heat in the middle. As the oven temperature at top and bottom can vary as much as 25°F from this setting, the positioning of shelves is very important. In general, heat rises, so the hottest part of the oven is at the top, but consult the manufacturer's handbook about your individual model.

Pans and dishes of food should be placed parallel with burners or elements to avoid scorched edges.

When baking cakes, there must be room for the heat to circulate in the oven around baking sheets and cake pans; otherwise the underside of the cakes will burn. If baking more than one cake in an oven that has back burners or elements, arrange the cakes side by side. If the oven has side burners, arrange cakes back and front.

Oven thermostats are often inaccurate and are unreliable at extremely high or low temperatures. If you do a great deal of baking or question the accuracy of your oven, use a separate oven thermometer as a check on the thermostat.

INDEX

(Volume 18)

S

Z

T

V W

Acknowledgments
Photographs by Fred J. Maroon on pages 30, 42, 45, 47, 49, 63, 64, 83, 112, 116 and 121. Other photographs by Michael Leale, Gina Harris and John Ledger.

NOTES

Notes